AF609173

Surrender to Your Truth

A Powerful Journey to Explore the Depths of your Soul and Awaken your Sexual Power

Kerry O'Sullivan

ISBN13:978-1-913728-33-5

authors
AND CO.

CONTENTS

DEDICATION

For all the powerful women standing in their truth
& for those who are ready to take that step.
Together we rise.

ACKNOWLEDGEMENTS

I have so many people to thank because without them I would not have finished this book.

Firstly, I would like to thank Mark. There are not enough words that can express my pure gratitude for you, especially over the last four years and the whirlwind we've been on. I love you so much darling, thank you for holding on through the crazy, for all those 'acts of service', for the all the nights of editing the book, for all you bring to our relationship and for holding me close.

My gorgeous Emily, my mini me, my everything. One day you will read this book and understand why writing this book meant so much to me. You are my world and my inspiration to keep going through it all. Joseph, thank you for your part in my growth and the mirrors you revealed to me. I love you both so much.

To all of my friends and family who have been my sounding board and support in this chapter to become an author, especially my fabulous assistant Natalie, Jennifer, Lisa, Ben, Ashley, Nicola, Helen, my neighbours, school friend mums and dads, Destination Inspiration mastermind family and anyone else who has heard me waffling on about every stage of the book process.

To all of my gorgeous clients, my goddesses and couples – I wouldn't be here without you. Thank you for trusting in me, for surrendering in your truth, for all the love, support and inspiration you gave me to write this book.

Amanda Heath – Thank you bringing my vision to life and creating the most phenomenal goddess painting for my front cover, you are amazing and I'll cherish our friendship forever.

Yvette Taylor – Thank for every part you have played in my journey so far and for writing the gorgeous Foreword for my book. I will forever be grateful for your friendship, love and support and for stopping me from running away from the part of me that has changed my life.

My best friend Jennifer Yellow Hat for our beautiful 20-year friendship and for creating me the most gorgeous vulva for the book.

To all my teachers and coaches that have inspired me personally and professionally and have held me through the depths of despair to the euphoria of my awakening; so much love for each and every one of you – Camilla Baker, Yvette Taylor, Gayatri Beegan, Harmony Isgold, Bayari Beegan, Sy and Ash Balderson, Elaine Yonge, Bynoi Desouza, Georgina Peard, Selwyn Warren, Lisa Bean, Lisa Johnson, Aimee Charlotte and the amazing Abigail Horne, Jane and the team at Authors and Co, who have held my hand through the birth of this book.

To everyone else, I've forgot to mention by name, you know who you are and I thank with all my love too.

FOREWORD

You hold in your hands the answer you've been asking for. There is always a reason the universe guides us to meet the right people at the right time.

It's an honour to watch someone wake up to their unique power. Seeing them go within to uncover who they are and expand that new sense of themselves into the world.

Meeting Kerry some four years ago, neither of us imagined what life would unfold; we never knew just how important we'd be in each other's lives. I'm so incredibly proud to know her and see who she has become and the massive impact she is creating in the lives of those she's touched. She is such an inspiration.

My name is Yvette Taylor; people know me as the creator of EAM – The Energy Alignment Method ®. EAM is a transformational self-help tool and internationally recognised complementary therapy. Through this work, I've also become an international best-selling author, speaker and coach. We lead a fantastic community of over 50,000+ people who are putting EAM into practice and making a big difference in their lives and the lives of others around them.

Kerry was one of the first mentors to train with me to use EAM, way back in 2017. Her powerful blend of Tantric embodiment, sexual connection and rediscovery work with EAM is inspiring to watch. I've watched her guide hundreds of people through this powerful work; I know you are in super safe hands. In her 15-year journey, working with hundreds of clients as a holistic therapist, Kerry has become well versed in the world of transformation. However, she has taken it to another level in the last four years, sharing her message with thousands. She is passionate about this fantastic work, and having seen her journey, I know she is never afraid to lean in, to explore the next phase; there is nothing she hasn't seen, heard, felt or experienced. It has been AMAZING to see the butterfly that has emerged.

Now, she is sharing this knowledge with you. To discover yourself and surrender to your truth, you have the steps to get there in your hands. Led by someone who has walked every step of the path ahead of you.

It may feel weird, strange or different, which means you are opening up into new territory, that is precisely where you need to be to change your life. If the answer to doing so were within your grasp already, you'd have found it. So trust the newness, take the steps, follow the practices and ideas Kerry has shared within this book. By the end, you will find yourself living in your truth and see your life in a whole new way. What better gift can you give yourself?

We both have a shared passion for empowering people to reconnect to themselves and live their truth, which is why I'm so excited to be introducing you to this book. Your energy is the key to it all; any challenges you face in life can be resolved holistically by working in the energy field.

My journey to self-discovery was rooted in sexual trauma. I was only 11 - 12 years old at the age my innocence was taken not once, not twice, but three times within six months. Tapping into that part of me became functional, disconnected, a tool, weapon, or something to others - never for myself, my pleasure, my desires or connection. Had it not been for the power of energy work, I would not be here today.

Let's face it, for many people our connection to our sexual selves has constantly been shamed, hidden, seen as rude, wrong, mistreated or used to exert or remove power from others.

We are rarely taught the powerful, sacred connection to ourselves, which can be found by tapping into this life-giving energy.

Inside this book, you will discover how to step into the person you truly want to be and surrender to your truth, explore how your energy systems work and integrate to create and shape your whole life experience, and discover simple energy practices which will allow you to get connected to yourself in a few minutes per day.

As you discover who you are and explore the timeline of your life, you'll find what shaped you, and you will uncover what held you back in life. As you find what those areas are, it means you'll be able to apply these powerful tools (one of which is

EAM) to let them go, so your past no longer shapes your present or future.

By exploring your past, your heart, mind, and emotions, you'll find the powerful elements that make you, well ... YOU!

When you understand what they tell you AND, even better, how to work with them, you'll see your life unfold in powerful ways as you connect with your true self.

In exploring the divine masculine and feminine, which is the foundation of all energy and life on earth, you'll understand and see where conflicts have arisen, or continue to arise, in your life. By learning to sink into your true archetypal self and connect, you'll fall into a new self-awareness and connection level.

Then we get to the juicy bit; your sexual power, your divine energy. Learn how to tap into your sacred energy and recognise the connection to your heart's desire, pleasure and awakening to loving yourself and every corner of your body in a whole new way.

With Kerry as your guide, you'll be ready to take this newer version of you into your relationships, so you can powerfully connect with others, communicate your desires, your needs and surrender to your true self. Put what you learn in this book into practice and see your life transform in the blink of an eye. I promise it will open your mind to the power of possibilities you have ahead of you.

This is the book you have been waiting for, with grounded, practical conversation, actionable exercises, no weirdness or ickiness - just support and experience from someone who is the living embodiment of 'doing the work'.

I'm so excited to see this book as I know how long it has been a part of her vision, and I know that together, the power of EAM, Tantric embodiment and self-exploration will create an orgasmic explosion of energy into your life; one you will never have dreamed could exist.

Now it is time to turn the pages, tune in and let Kerry show you the journey as you Surrender To Your Truth.

Yvette Taylor

Creator Of EAM - The Energy Alignment Method

Inspirational Speaker, International Best Selling Author,

Change Maker

THIS IS YOUR TIME TO STEP INTO THE PERSON YOU TRULY WANT TO BE

Imagine a world where you put yourself first, you knew how to step into your power and embrace everything you think and feel. You had the tools to empower you, so whatever life threw at you, you surrendered because you knew it would set you free.

Imagine a world where your light shined brightly, you felt happy, radiant and content through every cell of your body because you were living your truth and a life you desire.

Close your eyes now and imagine this; take a long deep breath and know it is possible, you can have it all.

Trust.

Believe.

Surrender.

If this feels like a way off for you, know that the more you look inside of yourself, more of you is revealed and that's when the magic happens. When you connect to the truth of who you are, you can meet yourself in what you need to connect to your power.

Just picking up this book, you have said YES to yourself. If you are scared, know you've got this and this is all part of the journey to Surrender To Your Truth, to accept all of you and connect to your inner power that is waiting to be ignited.

I'll start the journey by telling you a little bit about me and my journey. I had no idea I was numb. But I do remember the day it all changed, when I took that first step to do something just for me.

That first step is the beginning of something beautiful and if this is your first step, I celebrate you.

A little bit about me

My whole life I have dreamt of writing a book, but always thought no one would want to read it and that my life 'wasn't that interesting. I now know that my journey to my awakening and finding pure love for myself IS worth sharing, as I want to empower others to do the same; to love themselves exactly as they are because only then can we deepen our connection with others and shine our light in the world.

This book is part biography, with stories to inspire and motivate you. It's a story to set you free - from yourself, from your past and from whatever is stopping you from stepping into the beautiful, powerful woman you are.

My journey in life has been quite a whirlwind. I think I only appreciated recently how many things I have learnt along the way – at the grand old age of 41, I think I have had many life lessons already.

Awakening my sexual energy at 37 has been a life changer for me. For the first time, I felt so deliciously yummy, full of love, vibrancy, freedom and abundance and I have never looked back.

I feel so powerful; I feel it deep within my core. The freedom I have given myself to explore my sexuality has been such a blessing but, my goodness, it has been quite a journey to get here.

As I child, I was always different. I had boobs and curves from an early age and always got attention from men. In some cases, not good attention and those times from when I was younger, made me go inside myself. I suppressed everything I felt and I lived most of my childhood and adulthood being bullied and hiding my body behind big clothes.

Embracing my sexual energy has given me the power to move forward in my life, to leave the rat race behind and to concentrate on my passion to inspire and empower women to connect to themselves, to their truth and how they want to show up in this world.

Understanding self-love was my biggest learning achievement so far. Can you put your hand on your heart say you dedicate time to yourself every day? That you listen and acknowledge exactly how you are feeling and you do whatever it takes to nourish and love yourself?

All my life, I have never been good at this, never considered it before. I have always loved looking after others because it made me feel good about myself and without it, I didn't like myself very much.

I am here to raise the vibration of this planet, to inspire the masses. I know it's why I am here and it is the reason I get out of bed every day and have dedicated my life to always surrendering to my truth.

This book is a journey and is not something to rush. It's a gift of self-love; time for you to feel and connect to everything in YOU. The more you lean into it all, the deeper you will go.

The first time you read it, my invitation is to read it in order and if you feel called, do the exercises as you go. However, if you feel so intrigued about what is to come, by all means, read it all, but then promise yourself you will go back to the beginning and completed the exercises.

Get yourself a nice journal to accompany the book, one you can't wait to dive into whilst you explore the depths of your soul.

This is a book you can use forever, so once you've done all the exercises first time round, know you can dip in and out of the pages whenever you need reminding of the magic these pages contain.

This is your time:

Your time to up level.

To step into your Power.

To accept and embrace everything you are.

To connect to Love.

To awaken and embrace your sexual energy.

To connect to Pleasure.

To connect to everything that makes you feel alive from the inside out.

To Surrender To Your Truth.

I can't wait to guide you through this beautiful journey of deep self-love. Are you ready to turn the page? I am excited for you.

UNDERSTANDING ENERGY IS THE FOUNDATION FOR YOUR EXPANSION

It was over 14 years ago I discovered the world of energy, well consciously anyway. I started my journey in holistic therapies after the most profound experience on the top of a Spanish mountain. I had suffered from IBS my whole life and had no idea why. I saw an advert to go away to a retreat and help cure you from your illnesses. I had no idea what I was doing but was so desperate to understand why I was in crippling pain every day.

What followed was a week of fasting, daily juices and enemas, as well as an array of therapies and yoga sessions, including acupuncture and reflexology. This was such a long way from the life I led at home and I couldn't believe what my bowels released and how much crap my body was holding on too. There were a couple of pivotal moments in the week, I will never forget.

There was so much silence and I hated it. I remember one day, saying to the facilitator I needed to go for a run. My body was trying to slow down but I was trying to do what I had always done when things felt hard - run away, pound the treadmill, anything that stopped me feeling. It was only a small place but I ran up and down the roads like I was losing the plot. I was so desperate to squash down all the emotions that were bubbling in me. I knew I was being crazy but I was so scared of stopping. I remember the following day, sitting in the most beautiful room writing in my journal and knowing I was editing myself, I was not going to admit how I felt… absolutely no way!

At the end of the week, I treated myself to some treatments and had a beautiful acupuncture and reflexology treatment. A beautiful soul was treating me and made me feel so relaxed. He explained he was removing blockages in me and the needles help the flow of chi (energy) in the body. At the end, he left the room and told me to relax. I lay there frozen, with so many needles in me, and told myself to chill the Fuck out! It was so hard but I did. I felt myself go all warm and tingly, like something was moving in my body. I felt like the sun was shining down on me. I opened my eyes, there was no sunshine in the room and my body was alive. OMG, what is this?

I still didn't feel ready to embrace what was happening and what I was feeling but it was the start of something in me. It felt so incredibly healing, I knew I wanted to learn how to do this for someone else. It was always about others and how I could use what I experienced to help others. After this life changing experience, I went on to train in Indian head massage, reflexology and reiki, and spent the next 12 years healing others through the power of energy.

Everything is energy vibrating at different levels

And yep, you got it, totally forgetting about me. I wasn't ready for me yet.

My true awakening began in August 2016 when I left my 15-year career in media. It was such a hard decision as I loved my job, but it was all-consuming. I was a new mum and I felt like I was constantly running all the time, jumping from one thing to the other, with no time to breathe. I was on the hamster wheel and when I stopped, it felt uncomfortable, so I kept going. I'd had some challenging times in my career as I continually strived for more and loved to learn, to grow and expand all the time. I knew I was good at it too but I was surrounded by a lot of people that didn't see the potential in me and I think I drove them mad with my enthusiasm.

The real turning point for me came when one of my best friends was diagnosed with cancer. I had lost many people in my life before but this was a real shock. It was so close to home and made me realise how much your life can change in an instant and your whole world completely turn upside down.

I asked myself, "am I living the life of my dreams?" and I knew I wasn't. I loved living my life to the full but when my little one came along, it never felt the same. I didn't get the same buzz out of my job and I was always running from one thing to the next. Something had to change or I would never get off the hamster wheel of craziness. I yearned for a more chilled life at home with my family, but also had this real inner knowing that there was something more, I just had no idea what that was. So when I left my job, my whole world changed.

I remember the first week after I left, I was like a lost soul. My little one was at nursery and I had given myself a month off work as I felt like I needed time and space to transition from my old life into the new. I wanted time to be and to see what opportunities came my way. It is so important you create space if you want things to change, otherwise there is no room for the new things to fit in.

One day, I was in a coffee shop flicking through a magazine and thinking, what am I going to do with myself, and then I saw an advert to learn how to meditate. I made the call then and signed up to a five day 121 course the next day with my beautiful, now- friend, Camilla. I had no idea what impact this was going to have on my life. For the first time, I was in long periods of silence, well 20 minutes twice a day, but it felt like forever for someone that never had silence in her life.

Whilst in meditation, I started to have wild visions where I was acting out sexual fantasies, having sexual encounters with others. I remember saying to Camilla, is this normal? What is going on? She told me to sit with it and it would all become clear in time. It was all happening for a reason. I never had any idea what was going to happen next and that's when the unfolding of who I really was started to reveal itself.

Shortly after this, I discovered Yvette Taylor and The Energy Alignment Method® and realised this energy world was mind blowing. I signed up to a free 15-day trial, where we looked at different emotions every day, and I had the craziest experience. I was working on releasing anger towards my mum at the time, after a family row left me feeling annoyed. I worked on how this was making me feel. The next day, I lost my voice - and I mean completely lost it - for three days. I was unable to communicate with my mum at all and I had to deal energetically with all the emotions I couldn't express myself through my voice.

Responding through anger wouldn't have got me anywhere so this way, I calmed down and released the tension... and lost the ability to speak. Crazy, eh?!

From this experience, I realised the power we have over our energy and how quickly you can go from being angry to being speechless and losing the ability to speak.

Once you get it, it's a huge game changer. You have the choice of how you feel, how you react, how you think at any given moment. It's all energy, it's all moveable. You might be thinking, "yeah, right", but I am going to show you how in this book.

Once you understand energy and the acknowledge you can change it, there are no more excuses to stay stuck, as you know exactly what is going on. I know it can be annoying too, especially if you've been telling yourself you can't all your life.

It's easy to blame everyone else for what you have been through in your life and for the reasons you are stuck, but it's no one else's fault. You have the ability to change everything from what you are thinking, to how you feel about yourself and how you connect to others. The best thing is, it can be super quick if you listen and acknowledge what is really there. I never knew I wasn't awake. What a crazy concept; you can be alive but not be awake, but you may not know that you are numb until you know what awakened feels like. By the end of this book, you will feel more awake and this will be the beginning of a new chapter for you.

When I was numb, I never felt satisfied in anything I was doing. I was always looking for the next thing to make me feel happier. Although I was happy to a point, I never felt fulfilled and always felt like there was more. As humans, it's natural to grow and develop and I was rushing from one thing to next, hoping this next course might be the one I had been looking for.

Across this book, I will be sharing with you the steps that took me on my journey of awakening and how I then transformed my life and found my inner happiness. It all started with having more awareness of energy, which is the foundation to it all.

So let me explain about why understanding energy is super important in understanding YOU

Energy is what we are made up of, it's what everything around us and everything we touch is made from. It's life as we know it; millions of particles of energy which are continually moving, changing and evolving.

Everything is energy, vibrating at different levels, and we are all connected. You know when you think of someone and then they call you? That is no coincidence. 'It's because we are connected to each other energetically.

I never understood it, but knew I had the ability to move energy through someone. When I did my reflexology treatments, I felt energy move and I felt the power of bringing someone back into a place of alignment. To a place of feeling balanced. I loved that part of my job, the transformation. One of the frustrations I had was most of my clients put all the power in my hands and were waiting for me to 'fix' them each month, but as soon as they left, they carried on with life as normal, didn't do any of the things I suggested and went back out of alignment, waiting for their monthly fix to bring it all back. Believe me, I get it. That's what I had done my whole life. I thought I had to look elsewhere to 'fix me' and not once did I consider I could help myself, well not until the signs came very loud and clear.

I will refer to your energy a lot as understanding this is foundation of getting to know you. Once you know how to connect to your own energy, you can change, expand and channel it so it works for you. When you have mastered this for yourself, you can change the way you show up in the world and relate to others. You have the ability to change your energy in an instant, how amazing is that?!

In EAM, they speak about three main energy centres in the body, all with strong electromagnetic energy; the head, the heart, and the hara. I was so aware of the head as I had spent most of my life here, and the heart I knew was about emotions, but I had no idea what the hara was. Here is a little summary of each of them:

Head Energy - You probably recognise statements like "I am so in my head today". Your head is the energy of what's going on in your mind. It's all your thoughts and beliefs. Some of these, you may be consciously aware of and others you'll have no idea of or may choose to ignore.

Heart Energy- Your heart energy is your feeling energy, your emotions and your intuition. It's the home of love. That feeling you get in your heart, whether it be joy or pain, can be physically felt here.

Hara Energy - The hara is in the pelvis and this is the home of sexual energy, creativity and manifestation. It's where life is created in this world. It's an area that's hugely untapped and misunderstood and I can't wait to introduce you to more of the power this energy centre creates.

When all these centres are aligned and in flow with each other, that's when you are in your power, when you feel invincible and empowered and life flows beautifully. The decision making and action taking of the head is aligned to the connected, calm, sensual side of the heart and together with the passion and power within the hara, it gives you the boost and energy to live the life you desire.

Now let's go a little deeper and look at the chakras

The word Chakra is used to describe the energy centres within our bodies. They connect our physical and energetic bodies and are repeated across all layers of our aura. Having an understanding of these will help you to understand any blockages that may arise and also what they may be linked to energetically.

As you grow and develop, all the energy you create is stored within the chakra energy centres and sometimes they can get blocked (with resistance). This can affect the flow of energy, taking you out of alignment.

When you are in alignment, the chakras are fully open and spinning energetically as they should. When in resistance, they become smaller in size and energy and can get blocked. There are thousands of chakras but below is a summary of the seven main ones and how they relate to the body.

The Root Chakra

This is also referred to as the base chakra and is the foundation we build the rest of our life on. This chakra, which is red in colour, represents the basic elements of life: feeling safe, feeling like you belong, are protected. It can also concern basic needs like money and material possessions, which are linked to feeling secure.

When your root chakra is in balance, it will ground you to life like the roots of a tree. The stronger the roots, the more you will blossom above and feel more connected within your body. When this chakra is out of balance, it can make you feel unsettled and manifest physically in lower back pain, problems with the knees and hips and in relationships - you may be over obsessive with your lover or past lovers where you may have felt insecure.

A great way to balance this chakra is to bring your energy into a grounded place, so you feel more secure. My favourites are walking barefoot or going for a swim in open water.

The Sacral Chakra

This is the second chakra. It is orange in colour and encompasses the pelvis, reproductive organs, lower intestine and bladder. It is affected by thoughts and feelings around your sexuality, pleasure, addictions and thoughts about your appearance.

Issues of power and control can also be very present within this chakra. This chakra can be out of flow or have blockages if you have ever suffered any sexual trauma, or times when your boundaries have been pushed by a lover. Any shame and embarrassment from sex is also stored here. This can be with another or with yourself and whether you are comfortable in your sexual expression.

To help balance this chakra, being open around expressing your sexuality and surrounding yourself with positive and sensual people in your life can help this chakra expand.

The Solar Plexus

This is the third chakra and it is affected by thoughts and feelings around self-expressions, self-respect, confidence and control - especially around fears of losing control or being controlled by others. It's about understanding who you are and what you stand for as an individual.

If this is out of balance, you may feel like you don't know yourself or don't trust your actions. This is often the part of ourselves that we ignore.

A balanced solar plexus looks like the sun; it's yellow energy radiates from within you when you are truly connected to the essence of who you really are.

Listening to and trusting your intuition and gut feelings can connect you here.

The Heart Chakra

The heart chakra is the first chakra connected to spirit. It's connected to your emotions and is affected by your thoughts and feelings around compassion and unconditional love.

A cleansed and balance heart chakra has energy flowing through it. You are connected into feeling all emotions and the way you give and receive love, both by yourself and others. The heart is also a place that can carry resentment, guilt and grief, due to past experiences with love and denying your needs. This can cause blockages to feeling and to connecting to yourself and those you love.

Spending more time on self-love and letting yourself feel and embrace your vulnerability is key to balancing your heart chakra.

The Throat Chakra

The throat chakra is all about expression and your ability to communicate your truth. I like to call it being beautifully authentic. It sits between the head and the heart. When they are in harmony, you express yourself clearly and lovingly; when out of balance, you may become critical and judgemental.

The throat chakra can hold a lot of tension and blockages around speaking your truth, especially in sexual situations where you feel like you need to hold back in some way.

To open up this chakra, practice asking what you want in all situations. Even if you first feel uncomfortable, give it a go and see how it feels.

The Third Eye Chakra

This is the sixth chakra and is linked to your desire or reluctance to see the future. When in balance, you can see who you are, your vision and what your true calling is in life.

When out of balance, logic starts to take over and you may be recalling events in the past blocking you from moving forward without even being consciously aware.

Doing regular vision meditations can help you connect to your vision and improve your trust and intuition.

The Crown Chakra

This is the home of the ultimate orgasm and our connection and surrender to higher consciousness and divine energy. When you are connected through your crown, you are more open to receiving messages and trust the path you are on. You are also more open to divine energy and open to welcome in your guides and helpers as and when you need them.

Regular orgasms with yourself or others connect you to your divine energy. You can also meditate and spend time being still to deepen the connection too.

So how can we work with energy in our bodies?

I am now going to explain some fundamental tools I use to connect and move energy in the body. I can't emphasise enough, understanding these and using them on a daily basis will give you the time and space to connect to how you think and feel about anything. They are especially powerful when you feel like you are stuck or have a block. You can use these to expand and move the energy through your body.

Tantric Embodiment

I will explain later how I discovered the world of Tantra, as it's been a huge part of awakening my sexual power. A lot of people hear the word Tantra and think it means sex and yes, there is Tantric Sex, but I discovered Tantra when I was looking to be healed from my past sexual trauma. Tantric Embodiment is giving yourself permission to feel everything, to embody and embrace it all so it can move, expand and connect you more deeply to the emotional, sensual, spiritual and sexual powerful woman you are.

This type of embodiment work has helped me to be more present in any situation and more aware of how I am feeling. Embodiment work is a huge part The Goddess Awakening Journey®, my deep-dive, intimate group programme to explore the depths of you. There are weekly embodiment practices to delve deeply into your soul. Embodiment gets you out of your head and into your body and there is magic in the ability to move the energy through you.

There are three elements to Tantric embodiment which are key in facilitating energy flow throughout your body; breath, sound and movement. Do not underestimate the power of these elements, they may look simple on the surface but they magical.

Breath

Deep breathing is key to awakening your body. When you breathe deeply into your stomach, more tension is released. The more relaxed you become, the more the beautiful energy created will move around the body making you more balanced and alive. It's simple but we often forget how powerful it is to breathe.

Sound

This is about letting yourself express yourself through sound and letting whatever wants to come out be expressed. This could be bursting into song or making beautiful sensual sounds, whatever feels good for you. People sometimes struggle with this as there is so much conditioning around letting ourselves go. When we sigh, people ask what's wrong, but sighing is you moving energy out that wants to be expressed. The more connected we become, the more we will know what sounds our body is yearning to express. Relax and let it flow and tell yourself all is welcomed.

Breathe,
make sound,
& move the
energy
throughout
your body

Movement

Movement is key to move the energy around your body. It stops energy getting trapped and enables you to feel the energy everywhere. During the exercises, move in a way that feels good for you - stretch, shake, whatever your body is asking you to do. Move and feel the magic of the energy vibrating through your being.

Breath, Sound and Movement is something that is forgotten, especially when practicing embodiment. There is a great exercise coming up at the end of the chapter for you to practice using these.

The Energy Alignment Method®

The Energy Alignment Method® (EAM), is an internationally recognised complementary therapy created by one of my wonderful teachers and mentor, Yvette Taylor. It's a simple, yet transformational, five-step self-help technique designed to shift energy, thoughts and emotions so you can change what you see, feel or experience in your life. I was one of the first 26 mentors to train in this modality globally, which is super exciting and is a big part of the work I share in the world.

EAM is more than just another mindset tool; with it, there's no need to regurgitate the past or dig up memories. It's more than a manifesting tool; it's a way of life and I use it every day, even when I am on the go, in the shower, cooking the dinner and in the supermarket.

Throughout the book, I will be showing you some ways in which you can use EAM to explore and expand your energy. You've learnt about the powerful energy centres; the head, heart, hara and the seven chakras. Now, here are the three flows of energy to understand how energy shows up in you:

Receptive (In Flow) - When you are in flow or in alignment, life feels really easy. We are loving our day, our thoughts and emotions are positive, we feel content, happy and in control and feel connected to ourselves and others.

Resistance - This is when things feel like hard work and take a lot of effort. You may be experiencing emotions like blame, shame, anxiety and it normally means there is a conflict between your head (thinking) and heart (feeling).

Reversal - When you are in reversal, you can feel stuck and it's when there has been a shock or disruption in your energy.

The Five Steps of EAM

There are five steps to EAM and using the body as a pendulum. It's super helpful when you would like some more clarity on what's going on in your energy and understanding whether something is a yes or a no.

Step 1: Ask

This step is to give you clarity on what you need to shift. Ask your energy a simple question to see if it's something you need to work on. For example, 'Do I have resistance when I think about fully expressing myself?'

I am ready to receive

Step 2: Move

Your energy body will respond and give you the 'yes' or 'no' answer to the question you asked. Forward is usually 'yes' and backward usually 'no'. If you sway another way, check for energy reversals (more info on the bonuses page on this – www.kerryosullivan.co.uk/book).

Step 3: Experience

This step is all about assessing what's happening in your energy when you think about that subject. You can perform this step in multiple ways. Choose which is appropriate for you.

1. What happens to your energy? Describe the size/colour/shape/location, etc.
2. How many of something do you have? Use the sway to identify the number.
3. Which emotions do you feel?
4. Explore clarifying questions. Ask further questions to get more detail.
5. What do you see in your mind's eye? Describe the visual picture.

Step 4: Transform

Prepare and say your statement, 'I AM ready to release (whatever the subject). I release it from my energy in all forms, on all levels, and at all points in time.' Repeat this at least three times or until you can no longer feel the resistant energy. Remember to check it has been released by asking your sway before moving to step 5.

Step 5: Manifest

Prepare and say your statement, 'I AM ready to allow/receive/experience/think/feel (whatever the subject). I allow this into my energy in all forms, on all levels, at all points in time.' Repeat three times or more until you can feel it in your energy is in alignment and you sway forward.

I have included an EAM video demonstration of the five steps on the *bonuses page (www.kerryosullivan.co.uk/book)*

Connection Exercises:

1. Connecting and grounding to the here & now

A simple exercise for you to connect into the present moment and to listen to yourself is to take some time to connect to the earth. Earth energy is grounding and helps you feel connected and safe. This is a practice I do regularly, especially if I find my mind running away from itself and life becomes super busy.

- Go outside and find a nice area – take your shoes and socks off, close your eyes.
- Breathe in through your nose and imagine the earth energy coming up from the ground and into the soles of your feet.
- Breathe it in, all the way through every part of your being and then exhale out through your mouth.
- Stay with this for a few breaths, giving the heart time to slow down and get used to the simplicity of this exercise and for you to be still.
- Ideally this will always be done outside, even in the winter and it's so beautifully refreshing. But if this isn't

possible, visualising the ground of the roots of the tree as you inhale is just as powerful.

- I would invite you to do this 1-2 times a day, it doesn't have to be long but enough for you to feel the difference it makes.

2. Practice Tantric Breathing

I call it Tantric Breathing as you are using the three core principles I learnt in Tantra: breath, sound and movement. I remember the first time I learnt how to breathe like this; it felt uncomfortable, it felt so alien to me but once I got used to it, 'it became something I now do all the time.

Learning to breathe more deeply, allows you to drop into your body so you can release tension and activate your energy body.

Find somewhere comfortable and take a moment with yourself and softly close your eyes.

- Purse your lips as though you are going to drink through a straw.
- Take a deep inhale - in for three.
- Then open mouth and breathe out slowly for four to five breaths.
- Remember to allow yourself to make sound or move if you would like to express yourself in this way.
- Do this 4 -5 times and listen to your body - What do you notice? Do you feel calmer? Do you feel more awake?

3. Aligning your energy with EAM

EAM is such an amazing tool to get your energy aligned. Have a go at this simple practice using the five steps to align your head, heart and hara. You can use EAM to check in with each energy centre and see if they have resistance, release it and then align them.

- Using step one of EAM, ask your sway "Is my head, heart and hara in alignment?"
- If it's a yes, that's great and is something you can check in with every day but also check on whether you have resistance to doing the exercise as this may be affecting your answer. If it's a no, then check in on each of them individually.
- Do I have resistance in my head? Do I have resistance in my heart? Do I have resistance in my hara? If the answer is yes, then you can release the resistance using the five steps of EAM for each energy centre - also check in whether you need to delve a bit deeper, you may need a number of how much resistance you are holding there.

I am ready to release the resistance in my head, I release it from my energy in all forms, on all levels, at all points in time. Repeat this for each energy centre until all resistance has been released.

Don't forget to do your step 5 and align all the energy centres again once you have released it all.

I am ready to align my head, heart and hara, I welcome this into my energy in all forms, in all levels at all points in time.

4. Connecting to your chakra energy

Head over to the bonus book page (www.kerryosullivan.co.uk/book) to download this beautiful guided Chakra meditation to connect you to your chakra energy centres. It's a delicious meditation and perfect to start or end to your day.

WHO ARE YOU REALLY?

This is a big question and the question alone might make you want to run a mile. In The Goddess Awakening®, it always brings up all sorts of triggers, so if this makes you feel uncomfortable, it's ok, it's totally normal. It may have been sometime since you've asked yourself that question. I know I never did and it wasn't because I consciously avoided it, it never crossed my mind as something that was important.

So take a moment now, close your eyes, take a few deep breaths, put your hand on your heart and ask yourself:

- Who am I?
- Then ask - who am I really?
- How does this feel for you?

If the answer is you have no idea, the truth is, you do, she is in there. Maybe you've been hiding that part of you for a while and it's far away from the place you are right now. But if you never ask, how will you ever know?

The past - it's all part of my journey

When I started my EAM journey, we unpacked this question. I went back and looked at my whole life to understand all the parts of my life that had contributed to who I am today. Although you don't need to go over all the details of it, understanding how it impacts you now is a key part in you stepping into your truth and moving forward into your future.

If you thought back to your whole life from the moment you were conceived to where you are today, I bet you could give me lots of answers to the question - who are you?

- Who have you been in each part of your life?
- Have you been the same person your entire life?
- Do you know the times in your life where you may have lost your sense of self?
- Are you being yourself in your life now?

Even if you don't think about your past, if exploring these questions makes you want to run away, it's definitely something to explore because it's in your energy, and working on what comes up when you go there, will keep you moving forward.

Up until the age of seven, whatever we experience in our lives builds the foundation of what you grow up to believe is 'normal'. So the environment in which you grow up and the things you absorb will impact the way you think and feel and what conditions you place upon yourself. You can see how this can then play out for the rest of your life in how you give and receive love, how you communicate with others, what does 'wrong' and 'right' mean or how does it feel to be safe? I realise now how important it is for me to feel safe and, as I explained with the Chakra Energy Points, the root chakra is the foundation of everything. If there is any part of you that doesn't feel like you belong or you are not safe, it will impact everything.

Until the last four years, I had no idea my childhood impacted my life as much as it did. When I looked back on my childhood, I used to tell myself I didn't have a tough time; it was my little world and it was just the way it was. Over the last few years I have had to heal so much from my childhood, from all the times I felt scared and unsafe and internalised it. I always felt so blessed to have the opportunities I did and I thought I had a pretty normal upbringing.

Growing up, I lived in a two-bedroom maisonette in Peckham, South East London with my mum, dad and little sister, Clare. I used to think it was quite posh. In my bedroom, not only was there a fire door directly into next doors bedroom, I also had windows on to a roof and in the summer, I used to sunbathe out there with my friends.

My mum and dad split up when I was four years old. My dad was a drinker and they used to argue a lot about money and that he was drinking all the money down the drain. I remember the day it all came to a head, my mum and dad had been arguing and my mum had chucked something at my dad which cut his eye. I don't know what happened, but I remember my mum telling me and my sister to get ready, we were going to my aunty Vi's. As we left, I looked into the kitchen and my dad was crying. Our kitchen window looked out on to Queens Road Peckham train station and when we were waiting for the train, I could see my dad with his head on the table. I felt so sad and didn't want to leave him.

My dad lived with my nan for a while and we used to see him at the weekends. Shortly after, he met my step mum Bev and they got married and had my little brother and sister. Me and my sister were so excited to be bridesmaids at their wedding. We wore blue and black polka dot dresses with puffball skirts – I loved them and it felt so exciting.

My mum met my stepdad not long after she split up with my dad, and life became a bit crazy as he had three kids. They came to live with us in our two-bedroom maisonette so as you can imagine, it was a tight squeeze. We all lived in each other's pockets and it definitely felt hectic - the weekends we were at my dad's felt like a welcome break. I loved going to Crystal Palace footie with my dad, fun days out together, experimenting with Bev's make up and spending time with my little Brother and Sister. I used to get up really early and wait for the first sound of them waking up and then run in and get them up out of their cots. Life was always busy but I didn't know it any other way.

As a single mum, my mum always worked so hard to give us everything she could. We didn't have the designer coats and the best trainers, and sometimes it felt hard when I compared myself to my friends. Looking back on it now, we had so much love though and the best my mum could give us whilst she went through so much on her own journey.

My mum has bipolar, so growing up and being the eldest, I always felt it was my job to look after everyone. I stepped into this role from a very early age. I grew up quickly, getting my first job at 12, working at Millwall football ground in the food and drinks kiosks. If you know anything about Millwall and football, you'll know it was chaotic and could be quite ferocious at times. I felt so grown up, but when they let the crowds in, I always felt a nervous excitement, especially when I worked on my own. I loved having my own independence though and treating my mum to a bunch of flowers every week with my wages.

There was a pivotal moment I remember so clearly where my life changed forever. I think I was 15 years old. I don't remember exactly what happened but my mum was so upset. She had smashed some plates and she sat on the kitchen floor with her head in her hands and was rocking back and forth, crying her eyes out. I went down to the floor, sat behind my Mum and she leaned into me and sobbed. That image comes to me so often as the moment we switched roles and I decided, I became mum. Note there, the use of the word, I. My Mum never told me it was my role; it was something my 15-year-old self decided. I was so scared, but without hesitation, I took that part.

Around the same time, my mum had an operation and had to go into respite care for a few days, and my dad came to look after us. One night, after I'd gone to bed, I went downstairs and noticed all the lights were still on. I looked in my mum's bedroom and my dad was there on the bed. He looked drowsy and was making no sense. I saw the pill packets and beer cans and realised he had taken an overdose. I picked up the phone and called an ambulance. They arrived soon after and I watched as they pumped his stomach. At the time, I did what I had to do but now, through the healing I've done these last few years, I know I was petrified. I know he was in a bad place too, as his marriage had broken down, but I was still so confused why my dad would do such a thing when he was meant to be looking after me and my sister.

What followed was years of turmoil as my mum's life broke down and she ended up in mental hospitals. God, it was so hard. I remember visiting my mum and always trying not to cry as I had to be strong for her and my sister. I didn't understand why it was happening and desperately wanted my mum to be better. My dad remarried for the third time and I remember finding that really hard at the time because we had started to become close and all of a sudden someone else was in his life and I felt like I was fighting for his time.

For so many years, I felt so angry towards my mum and dad because I felt I didn't have 'normal' parents. I think it all changed when I left for university. I couldn't wait to move away. I was desperate to start a new life and Stoke-on-Trent felt like a million miles away from London. When I look back, I think me leaving was a catalyst in my mum's mental health breaking down. I don't blame myself but I know I was running away from the life I had at home. I remember one day getting back from university and walking past the pay phone in the hallway of my hall of residence and one of the boys shouting out "your mum called and said to tell you as far as she is concerned you are dead". They were laughing their heads off and as I ran up the hallway, shouted "she is nuts". I went back to my room and sobbed my heart out. I was trying so desperately to hold it all together and hide this from my new life in Stoke. I couldn't understand why my Mum was so unwell; how could she say these things to me when she was my mum? Whist I was at university, my mum's breakdown led to her selling the family home and moving to Ireland. My sister moved into a hostel. We used to write letters to each other. I think we were both so used to surviving that we just got on with our lives. It was so hard being away from my sister but I knew I had to stay. Whilst everyone was rushing home in the holidays, I made my excuses and stayed on and worked at Safeway. I was lonely. I desperately missed my mum but did anything to try and stop myself from feeling the heartache I was experiencing.

In the summer holidays, I went to visit my mum in Ireland. She came to pick me up from the airport and I was so shocked when I saw her. Her hair was shaven off as she was convinced she had cancer. I sat there for ages before she noticed me and I was trying to stop crying. I never forget the rage in her eyes. It wasn't long before she lost it with me as I told her she didn't have cancer and the doctors had confirmed it. She started screaming at me and put her foot down on the accelerator. We were driving straight towards a lorry that had just pulled out to turn in the road. I screamed at her, she slammed on the brakes and we went flying across the central reservation, back around the lorry and she carried on driving and screaming at me like nothing had happened. It was awful. As soon as we pulled off the motorway, she told me to Fuck off, got out the car, threw my bags at me and drove off. I hadn't been to this village for years but somehow I managed to walk through the town and find my stepdad's family's house. I said who I was and they let me stay. More of the same happened over the next few days and I went home distraught, thinking I would never get my mum back again.

Part of my awakening has been connecting to the pain of feeling so scared and yearning for my mum and dad to be there for me, and also knowing it was ok to feel like that, giving myself permission to feel it so it could move through me. We had the most beautiful childhood in a lot of ways but as I became a teenager, it changed and by connecting to this pain, it has allowed me to forgive them as I know they were on their own journeys as well.

My mum is a big part of my life now and after all the ups and downs, our relationship has blossomed over the last few years. I realise how alike we are. I used to think her talk of spirit and angels were because she had Bi Polar. She told me stories about the night I was conceived and when she was pregnant with me, she knew I'd be special. At the time, I thought she was barmy. I know now, she gifted me with my connection to spirit and I love to hear all her stories. My mum is my inspiration to survive and, after all we've been through together, I know through my own healing, that I help her too and I am so grateful for her presence in my world. My dad and I still see each other, not as often as I'd like but he is happy and that feels good. His wife Sylvia was a blessing for my dad in him turning his life around and for that I am grateful.

Over the years, I have had so many wonderful women step in to look after me when my mum and dad couldn't be there:

My aunty Vi; she had always been our rock, through it all. In all my memories of growing up, Vi was always there. My aunty Vi is who I go to for tough love, no messing. She tells me what I need to do and I love her so much for that. I tell her all the time but I don't think she realises what a blessing she is to me, my sister and my mum.

My darling Olive, my mum's best friend and neighbour, who I lost a couple of years ago. I spoke to her all the time and lived with her when my mum sold the house. She was such a good listener and always told me how proud of me she was. I am so glad I always told her how much she meant to me, especially when she got dementia and I knew I was losing her. She couldn't speak much towards the end but I knew she could hear me. I felt her spirit with me that day and I still do.

In 1999, on my gap year from university, I went to live in Vancouver, Canada. My mum was in St Clements Mental Hospital. I remember saying goodbye. She gave me a panda teddy to look after me that I still sleep with today. When I look back, I had no idea how I left. I squashed everything down. I was desperately trying not to feel. In my first job, I met my beautiful Betty, who I now call my Canadian Mum. A huge lover of Londoners, we made friends straight away. Her heart has always been so huge and I always feel her love. I don't remember saying how much I missed home and missed my mum, but she knew. She took me under her wing and looked after me. We became great friends and she has become such a special part of my life and been there, through it all, over the last 21 years. I love being her English Daughter, she means the world to me.

My little sister, Clare. I know she doesn't realise how much she means to me. We've held on to each other through everything growing up and now, although we still have our little squabbles, our love is deep and when it comes down to it, we are always there for each other.

These amazing women have all played such a part in my life and I will always be forever grateful for their love and holding. I couldn't have got through it without them.

I yearned for a place I could call home but then always seemed to run away from what I knew was home as subconsciously, I was always looking for more. I went to university, miles away from home in Stoke-on-Trent. On my gap year, I decided I would go to Canada on my own. At both times, being driven by the drive in me to succeed and telling myself there was no time to be scared, go, go, go!

I met some wonderful lifelong friends on my Canadian gap year adventure, had my heart broken, dated someone who turned out to be a criminal on the run and I came back to the UK, to life as it was, with a bump. I was expecting everything to have changed, but nothing had really. My friends were still doing the same things, my mum was still unwell and off I went, back to University, feeling disappointed that nothing had changed when inside I felt quite different. The next few months were wild, fuelled with drunken nights, sex, taking drugs, losing loads of weight as a result and, as I thought then, living life to the full. I had no idea what I was doing was still squashing down anything I was feeling.

I came back to London at Christmas. I stayed with Olive and was feeling so lost. I threw myself into the Christmas Festivities and on Christmas Eve, I ended up meeting a man who would become my future husband. The bizarre thing was, at the time, my childhood sweetheart who had totally broken my heart years before, told me he was interested in me again and it felt so good. I wanted him too and I dared to admit it. So here I was, Christmas Day, feeling a bit lost, with two men in my life saying they'd like to date me. WTF?! Honestly my whole life, I hadn't been noticed by men in the way I'd like and here I was with a choice to make. I chose my now ex-husband, as he felt like the safer option in a time when I was yearning for love and petrified of having my heart broken again.

I fell head over heels for him and couldn't quite believe a man had wanted me and it was for more than for sex; it was for all of me. It was new territory for me and I was so besotted with him, I even considered giving up university as I felt like I never wanted to be apart from him. My friends, Emma and Jenny, kept calling and telling me I needed to come back, but it felt so good to feel wanted and I never wanted to leave. I finished university and we went off traveling around the world together. There was so many ups and downs and a moment in Australia where we nearly broke up. I knew deep down we weren't good for each other, but was desperate not to be on my own. I found out he was having intimate conversations with a woman in the UK whilst we were away and even though it hurt so much, I thought I was so lucky to have him and couldn't imagine life any other way. Eight years later, he proposed. I remember being so shocked and thought I'd be elated but wasn't. A year later, we were married in Canada. Another year later, he came home and said he didn't love me anymore.

My whole world came crashing around me.

He never admitted it at the time but he was leaving me for a younger model. I remember thinking this can't be happening to me and I went into complete victim mode, totally disempowered. He never wanted to try and make it work and was adamant it was over. When I look back, there had been so many warning signs over the 10 years I was with him. The relationship wasn't healthy for either of us; he was going outside of our relationship but I ignored it. I was so paranoid all the time and even on the day of the wedding, I was on a beach in Vancouver crying, thinking I'm sure I am not meant to feel like this on my wedding day? I was always on edge in the relationship. I felt jealous of other women he spoke with and was always suspiciously looking on his phone. I'd find things and he would tell me it was in my head or it was my fault he was being tempted by other women. I pushed it all down and kept going, pushing myself at work, trying to do everything but actually listen to what was really going on. We had such awful, vile arguments and used to rip each other to shreds. I had no love for myself, so why not let someone talk to me in this way?

The morning he left me, I remember begging him to not leave me. I was on the floor and he was standing above me. I begged him 'please don't leave me, I can't cope on my own, I need you'. I never forget it, he looked at me and said 'Look at the state of you. You are pathetic. Why would I want to be with someone like you?'. I had totally lost myself and the pain was unbearable, I felt like my whole world had exploded. I was 30 years old, married with a mortgage, about to start trying for a baby and then, in that moment, it was all over. I didn't think I would ever cope again.

I was broken.

The worse part of it is I was telling myself, you have to be strong. He had a huge family that I loved dearly and it had taken me years to get used to being in such a close loving family unit, I felt like I had lost more than him; I'd lost everything. I had a couple of days off work, spent the day with my friend, Alex, crying my eyes out and then told myself right that's it, enough of this, you need to move on. This was a pattern I'd played out my whole life, to dust myself off and keep going. I went back in a few days later for an important meeting we had with the CEO. It was a big deal. I remember telling myself, you get your arse in there, don't let this stop you. My colleagues looked at me in horror when I arrived I the office and suggested I popped a bit of make up on, I looked awful.

I am ready to be me

For months after, I threw myself into the gym, I ran for hours on the treadmill, got so busy doing anything to numb what I was feeling. I cried my eyes out the minute I got up and the moment I got in the door from work and those bits in between, I acted. I remember so many nights, binge watching Prison Break and staying up for hours, before I physically couldn't keep my eyes open. My beautiful niece was only a few weeks old and it was such a lovely distraction from the heartache I felt when I was at home. One of my friends suggested I speak to someone whose husband had left her. I didn't know this woman and can't even remember her name but that conversation gave me hope. I remember her saying 'you will get through this'. I didn't believe her at the time but slowly, I start to pick myself up and begin living again.

Only a few months later, I signed up to online dating and had the wildest time meeting people from all walks of life. I felt like I was in a game show; how many people could I meet in a week and what mask was I going to wear today? I had no idea who I was anymore. For 10 years, I had been in a relationship and here I was, in the big wide world and wondering who the hell I was really?

So my lovelies, as you can see from the stories I have shared with you, even at the age of 30, I had no idea who I was. I know I was in there somewhere, but I had so many masks, so much supressed trauma, and I never gave myself time to breathe and ask myself how I was and what I needed to make myself feel safe.

I never asked my inner child how she felt and know I would have learnt quite a lot from starting that conversation. But I also know I wasn't ready then. You have to be ready.

So if you are, let's start exploring your timeline and start the conversation with your inner child and see what she has to say:

Connection Exercises:

1. A timeline of your life

a) This is a great exercise to take a view on all of your life up until now. Get a blank piece of paper and draw a line in middle with 0 at one end and your age at the other and then mark 5 year increments, or there abouts, in the middle.

Take a few breaths with yourself and think, if my life was a story:

- What would be the main parts of your life?
- What have been the pivotal moments in your life?
- What Key events have happened that you know impacted your life in some way?

This can be as detailed as you like – think of it as the highlights of your life and it's useful to mark all the parts of you think of as positively impacting you at the top and those more challenging elements of your life at the bottom.

If you know anything about your time in the womb, include that too as it's all part of your journey.

b) Using EAM, go through and ask if you have any resistance to release from each of these parts of our life. Do this for both the positive and challenging times and transform the energy around them using the five steps (details in Chapter Two).

2. Starting the conversation with your inner child

Grab your journal, get comfy and take a few tantric breaths before you begin and let's get to know the inner child in you:

- As a child, I would spend time daydreaming about...
- When I was little, I dreamt of being…
- Growing up, I loved to…
- As I child, I spent so much time wondering…
- When I spend time with children now, it feels…
- If I could be a child again for one day, I'd …

WHAT ARE YOU RUNNING AWAY FROM?

As you have seen from my story so far, I spent a lot of time running away from what I was feeling as I didn't dare go there. Fear of going there is really common so you are not alone. All the questions, emotions and memories can be enough to stop you connecting to your truth. The exploration in the last chapter may be stirring some emotions in you and if you are ready, in this section, we are going to delve a litter deeper.

If you need some time to integrate what's coming up already, take it. This is not a reason to never pick this book up again though. This is the next step, to start listening to you and what's going on.

If you are here and ready to move on, we are now going to explore your thoughts, beliefs and emotions and some of the reasons why you might try and shut them down when they get too much. Being aware of this part of yourself, is connecting you to your inner essence and to the core of who you are.

If you don't truly love and know yourself, you disconnect to life, disconnect to those around you and this can leave you feeling stuck, like you are going around in circles and never moving forward.

When I was in this place, I remember NEVER feeling fulfilled in anything, I was always searching for the next thing to do: What else could I do in my life? Who could I help? What could I learn? I did everything that stopped me from getting to know who I was. I had so much fear of knowing who I was. Would it change my life? What would happen? All of these "what ifs" kept me avoiding going there for years. If this is you, know that I get it. But there is a freedom that comes when you start to take control over what you think and feel. The more aware you are, the closer you'll be to living the life you desire.

When your body shuts down and stops talking to you, there is always a reason and if we throw fear of knowing into the mix, then it can make you avoid the work all together.

How can you love your life if you haven't even connected to who you are?

The real you is in there and has never left your side. It maybe she is hiding and in time, she will most certainly come out to play but first, you need to figure out what's really going on.

It can feel soooooo scary, but if you don't, what's the alternative?

Living a life being totally disconnected and unfulfilled is no fun for anyone and certainly not for you. You deserve it all in life, beautiful one. Throughout this journey, I am going to show you how you can do this from a place of empowerment.

Don't wear a mask - it hides who you really are

So what happens when you start to listen?

When you start to listen, you become more aware of what you are thinking and feeling. At first the stillness can feel so busy. Your mind wakes up, it's jumping up and down thinking wow, this is a first, let me give her everything, in case she never stops again. Maybe your mind has never been given the space before and when it does, it thinks great, let's get these thoughts moving. This can often feel frantic, not make much sense and feel like a load of noise.

Quite often, this is when we switch in to busy mode and do anything we can to avoid listening, or even trying to calm the mind down - especially if you don't like what you are hearing. This can then lead you to do whatever you can to supress it and make it shut up! Already I can see you nodding your head thinking – OMG, she knows me!

Think about how you might supress your mind when you don't want to hear what it is saying. Below is a list of popular ways to do this and the crazy thing is, a lot of the time I bet you are not consciously aware you are avoiding listening to your mind:

- Scrolling through social media – think about how many hours you spend mindlessly scrolling, finding something to fill that gap.
- Watching TV, especially box sets that go on a continual loop and take you somewhere else.
- Throwing yourself into your work and telling yourself you are so busy ALL of the time.
- Sex – continually needing the release so it takes the edge off of how you are actually feeling.

- Eating especially moreish things like chocolate and crisps
- Alcohol – oh this is a good one to numb the mind from what is going on. It can also have the opposite effect too and get it all out but, not necessarily in an empowered way

So come on, own up? Do you do any of the above? And did you realise you may have been supressing your mind by doing so? We are going to look more closely at this in the connection exercises to identify anything you may have been doing to shut yourself up.

So do you know your own mind?

What I mean by this is do you listen to your thoughts and do you know if they serve you and are beneficial to your growth and development? Do they make you feel good or make you feel icky and awkward?

Most of my life, I had no idea what I was thinking, let alone whether they were good or negative thoughts. I knew I liked to keep going. I love to live my life to the full but I am so aware now of my thoughts all the time, which can also be a bit annoying too as I have a choice of whether I actually want to ignore them or acknowledge them so I can learn from them.

Listen to them all as they are all YOU and part of who you are.

The body is super intelligent and what happens when you continually supress your thoughts is they get louder and louder and can even manifest into illnesses within your body. Every illness is linked to an emotion in your body and when I started to understand this, I knew how much power I had over how I felt and even how I healed when I got sick.

If you are someone that gets continual headaches or your body feels tired, these are all linked to your thoughts and emotions. It's your body's way of letting you know to slow down and take time to connect to yourself, and the more you ignore them, the louder the body's cries become.

I will show you how to listen in the connection exercises, but the first thing you need to know is you always have a choice. When you let your mind rest and fall into silence, you then get to know you - all of you. The thoughts will come and you can listen to what you hear. Is it something that lights you up or does it make you feel uncomfortable? The parts that scare you, the parts that you run away from are the parts that you will really grow from. That is where the magic is.

You can move through it all – you've totally got this.

It was only four years ago that I realised how much I was still running away from everything I was thinking and feeling; when I started to listen to what was going on within me.

In November 2017, I had been on my EAM mentor training retreat in Morocco. It was a week of shifts and transformation and deep inner work but it was also the start of the healing of my trauma, when my body started to connect to what it had held on to for over 15 years. It was overwhelming and I ended up passing out one day because it got too much. After some fabulous TLC from the team, I left early, as planned, to return to a fundraiser we had organised for my friend, Helen. I remember driving to the venue and feeling sick, crying my eyes out but knowing I had no time to deal with this now, I had to put my face on and stand alongside my friends, hosting the night.

The next day, I kept going. I went to visit Helen and I knew she was transitioning. It was heart breaking as I never thought she would actually leave us. I was giving her some reiki and all of a sudden, she opened her eyes, sat up and said "thank you for all you've done for me in my life, I love you". She then laid back down and went back to sleep. I looked at her mum and we both knew then she was leaving us. My god, I will never forget that moment.

As I left her house, I kept going - running around, keeping myself busy, busy, busy, never ever letting myself stop and even contemplate what I was feeling.

The next day, we were running around doing errands and when we got home, I had stopped for the first time in days and I started to feel out of sorts. Within a few hours, I was lifeless and was rushed into hospital with suspected meningitis.

I remember seeing the look of panic in Mark's face as I couldn't remember my name or my date of birth. I thought I was living in a different year and I was slowly going offline.

I could see everyone staring at me - Emily saying "Mummy are you ok?". I remember trying to explain to the doctors I'd been working on my energy, had lots of trauma memories coming up and this was likely to be connected. He thought I was crazy and had totally lost my mind.

Energetically, my body was shutting down. The events from the last week were too overwhelming and I was checking out. I had spent the last two weeks trying to run away from my thoughts, from my body's cries to slow down and it had given up. I was put into quarantine and had a week of lumbar punches and scans. It was crazy.

I also lost my dear friend Helen to cancer that week and I felt like my whole world was crashing in around me again. I kept running.

I came out of hospital and I still wasn't listening. Only two weeks later, I did a 5k Santa race, even though I felt so unwell. I still hadn't learnt. I was pushing through, keeping going and it was only when I saw a recent Facebook memory, I realised how terrible I looked. I did everything I could to stop myself from feeling and instead went into a spin of crazy, trying to numb the pain.

Around the same time, I was in my yearly soul choir, which totally filled me with joy. We do six weeks of practice and then a performance at the end. I bloody love it and it totally lights me up.

Do you remember the song; I Believe I can Fly by R Kelly? This is a very special song to me for so many reasons.

When it came to the auditions, I thought I'd give this song a go. After I sang, everyone looked at me and said, "wow and you weren't even going to audition for that one". No one knew what was happening in my life. I never told anyone. A week later, I found out I had the solo and it was the second verse. It was so apt for what I was feeling and I felt every word. Singing it with 120 backing singers was out of this world and an experience I will never forget. I felt like I had my Mariah Carey moment. It was phenomenal!

Here are the words:

See I was on the verge of breaking down

Sometimes silence can seem so loud

There are miracles in life I must achieve

But first I know it starts inside of me

If I can see it, then I can be it

If I just believe it, there's nothing to it

I believe I can fly

I believe I can touch the sky

I think about it every night and day

Spread my wings and fly away

I believe I can soar

I see me running through that open door

I believe I can fly

I believe I can fly

I believe I can fly

Read the words again and really take them in as it almost sums up my journey to awakening and where it all started and for me. Oh my goodness, it was so painful to listen but I was so desperate to be set free and to learn to fly.

Without silence, I would never have known what was going on within me, what pain I was experiencing, what I was actually thinking about anything. I never gave myself time to listen to me.

I would never have known silence was loud - well it was actually deafening for me. When I silenced myself, my mind woke up and I wasn't interested in listening to it even though at times it was screaming at me to listen. Even in social situations, I would fill every gap with chatter; there was no space, no gaps, everything was filled but I genuinely thought this was how I liked it. I used to say out loud how I loved to be busy. I was even featured in my graduate magazine for university and I said I like stress because it keeps life interesting. How funny is that? I thought it was normal to feel stressed all the time.

Silence changed my life, from the moment I started to meditate. This is the place where it all begins because if you can't do that, how will you ever know who you are?

I have never felt beautiful, not deep down inside like I do now. I still have lumps and bumps but the beauty I feel is so much deeper than my body, it's deep into my heart and soul and it's like I have a calmness and stillness around myself that I have never experienced.

You do know the real you, she has never left your side

Your emotions – what are you feeling?

Maybe you have no idea how you are feeling. Or perhaps you know you've have been avoiding how you are feeling for a very long time.

Sometimes, you can be so far from who you really are, you have no idea how you feel, let alone what the emotions are. You may have spent your entire life telling yourself you have to be and act a certain way, so the emotions you feel have been suppressed. When was the last time you actually asked yourself – how am I feeling today?

When you get in to the pattern of running away from feeling, the emotions get pushed away. And when this happens time and time again, the body can become numb to the emotion so you don't feel anything.

If this resonates with you, know it is also normal to feel scared of going there. This is probably one of the biggest reasons why my clients feel so sick when they join my programmes. They are scared of what will happen when they open themselves up and whether will they be able to cope.

It's also the reason why I ran away from my emotions for so much of my life.

Leaning into everything you feel is the beginning of setting yourself free from anything that is holding you back from being even more fabulous.

This is also a practice though, and knowing, trusting and accepting things will always come up, but to be in your goddess energy, you embrace all of you. When you lean in to pain, you gain an understanding of what is going on; the thoughts, the emotions and the patterns that show up time and time again. It's your energy's way of letting you know the patterns are still there; they come up because they are ready to be set free. The more you set yourself free, the higher you rise, connecting more deeply to your goddess power in the process.

Understanding your emotions

Emotions are energy in motion. Electromagnetic energy is transmitted through your heart and as it moves, it gathers momentum. It's important to understand emotions have a vibration and an intensity, depending on how you are feeling. Negative emotions, like fear and overwhelm for example, are low vibrating emotions but feel intense. Negative emotions feel heavy, intense and leave you with low energy. Everything feels slow and tough to move through.

Positive emotions, like love and freedom, have a high vibration and flow through you. They are light and fast and when you're connected to these high vibrating emotions, you feel light and free, like you can achieve anything. How you are feeling will determine whether the vibration is high or low and this has a direct impact on your energy levels too.

You experience emotions every day and they can be enhanced or triggered depending on who you are with, how in flow you are, how much sleep you have had... so many factors can influence these and our reaction to EVERYTHING.

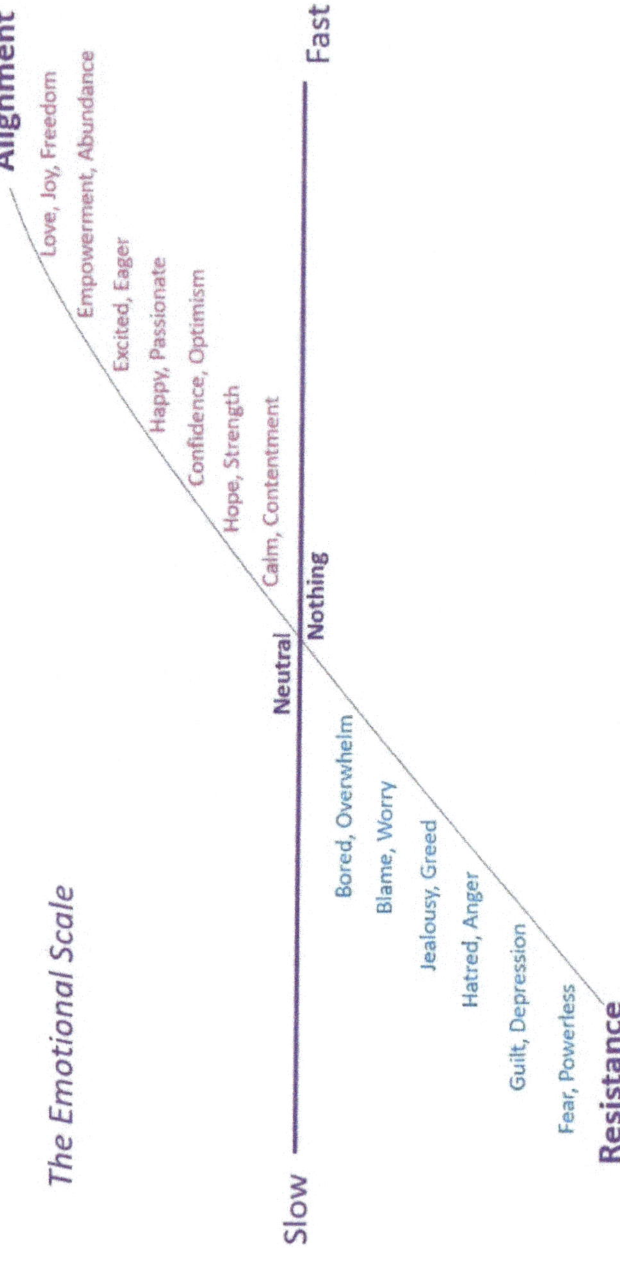
The Emotional Scale
Alignment
Love, Joy, Freedom
Empowerment, Abundance
Excited, Eager
Happy, Passionate
Confidence, Optimism
Hope, Strength
Calm, Contentment
Neutral
Nothing
Bored, Overwhelm
Blame, Worry
Jealousy, Greed
Hatred, Anger
Guilt, Depression
Fear, Powerless
Resistance
Slow
Fast

The Emotional Scale

The emotional scale is a great way to understand your emotions and to understand the difference between the high and low vibration emotions. Love is the highest vibration emotion (right hand side at the top of the scale) and fear is the lowest vibration emotion (left hand side and bottom of the scale)

Your emotions are so powerful and can be extremely addictive as your body can get used to feeling the same. This is why sometimes, when you feel like you've dealt with something, it comes back to bite you on the bum. When you've felt the same emotion a lot, the body creates a pattern and an imprint on your energy. The body feels comfortable defaulting to that emotion as it has been there many times before.

You can spend so much of your life suppressing emotion without even realising it, so when you give yourself permission to feel it, it opens you up to feel more of the higher vibrating emotions too.

Living life in alignment feels great, but it doesn't mean you will never feel resistant emotions. Being aware of them is key. When you keep yourself super busy or ignore your resistant thoughts or feelings, they stay in your energy and can manifest into a pattern. But the pattern can definitely be released and the more your emotions and energy are in high vibrational states, this then becomes the norm.

Are you listening to your mind & body?

How shock and trauma can affect your ability to feel

I had no idea I was numb and until four years ago, I had no idea I had deep rooted trauma affecting my ability to remember what had happened in my past.

A shock to your energy can cause your body to shut down and become numb to feeling what's really there. For me, this started when I was young and I pushed it away.

Trauma can occur due to a distressing event, witnessing something traumatic or physically experiencing something that at the time, you may not have fully digested. This then becomes an imprint to your energy and if you never go there and process it, can leave you feeling anxious, stressed or have the complete opposite effect and leave you feeling numb.

Numbness is so expansive and means so much. It is normally protecting you from the emotions and/or feelings that you do not want to feel. But the more you connect to it and send it love, the more it starts to soften so you can start to see what is beneath it.

Connection Exercises:

1) What are the thoughts you are aware of?

- Close your eyes and take three deep breaths and allow your mind to rest for a moment.
- Have a think of three thoughts you have repeated this week. It could be anything you say to yourself all the time, don't worry if nothing comes at first, give it time and enjoy the silence until something pops into your mind.

- Now take each of these thoughts individually and jot them down in your journal. Using EAM, check in with the sway and ask the following questions:
- Is this thought serving me?
- Is this thought disempowering me?
- How many times have I thought this?
- Is it a pattern? Check in on these.
- Make note of the answers and then release them using the 5 steps of EAM. For example, if you had the thought "I'm not good enough" and the sway identified it was not serving you and you had thought it 500 times, you would release as follows: "I am ready to release these 500 thoughts that I am not good enough, I release these from my energy, in all forms, on all levels, at all points in time," and repeat this until they have all released.
- In your step 5, you would then manifest how you would love to feel. For example, I am ready for myself to feel wonderful, inspiring, happy and calm, I welcome these beautiful thoughts and feelings into my energy in all forms, on all levels, at all points in time."
- If it's a pattern, you would release it in the same way. "Do I have a pattern of thinking I am not good enough?" If the sway says yes, you can release the pattern as follows: "I am ready to release this pattern of thinking I am not good enough, I release it from my energy, in all forms, on all levels at all points in time." And don't forget to do your step 5 as that is where the magic happens as it's bringing in all the positive thoughts.

Silence connects you to your truth

2) Take some to reflect on the following

- Make a note of some of the ways you numb yourself. Even though you may not be consciously aware you are numbing or avoiding listening to yourself, know it's likely to be playing a part in you listening to yourself more.
- What emotions do you know you supress in some way or find hard to express? Look at the emotional scale as this may help you identify what emotions they are and if not, sway on it with EAM.
- Can you think of a time in your life when you were ill and your body cried out so much you were forced to stop? And when you did, did you acknowledge why?

3) An embodiment practice to listen to the body

- Take a moment now. Close your eyes, take a few deep breaths, place a hand on your heart and ask yourself:
- Am I taking time every day to connect to who I really am?
- How does it feel to ask? Did it feel awkward or did it feel nice to take a moment?

Like with all this work, everything you experience whenever you ask yourself a question or do some embodiment work is important. You have to always remember it's your experience; there is no right or wrong and when we remove any goals or expectations around something happen, it allows whatever is there to show itself.

LEARNING TO DANCE WITH MASCULINE & FEMININE ENERGY

I had no idea about the power of energy when I started this journey, let alone what it meant to be in my masculine or feminine energies. It has been so useful understanding all the different parts of myself and how I relate with others.

Regardless of whether you are in a male or female body, you will have both masculine and feminine characteristics. They nourish each other, they both have a wounded and divine aspect and there is so much depth to them both. The wounded part comes from ego, your head energy. This is normally surrounded by fear and is darker and of lower vibration. The divine connects you to a higher vibrational energy from source and for me, feels beautifully sacred and powerful.

Being aware of these behaviours and patterns can help connect you more deeply to your truth as you expand and evolve into the person you are becoming.

I embrace all of me, the light and the dark

Below are some of the characteristics of the wounded and divine aspects of the masculine and feminine:

The Wounded Masculine: Controlling, aggressive, unstable, abusive, withdraws, avoids.

The Divine Masculine: Deeply present, focussed, honest, accountable, confident, logical, supportive, has integrity, takes responsibility.

The Wounded Feminine: Insecure, needy, co-dependent, inauthentic, over emotional and spends lots of time in victim mode and has weak boundaries around her own self-worth.

The Divine Feminine: Intuitive, grounded, supportive, vulnerable, authentic, surrendered, empathetic, compassionate, trusting, magnetic, expressive and in flow.

Do you recognise yourself in those characteristics? Be aware, you will move between these depending on your energy, the time of your life and who you are with. Having an understanding of these aspects of yourself and why they are here can take you from a place of the wounded into the empowered place of the divine.

When I think back to my life, especially before I started in the self-development space, I was most certainly living most of my time in masculine energy. This stemmed from my childhood and the role I took on to look after my Mum and everyone else that came into my life; always feeling the need to do, focussing my energy on always doing something, keeping myself busy with other people and trying desperately to fulfil something in me. I was so focussed on trying to make myself feel better, I was rarely present, not to the here and now. I was jumping from one thing to another all the time and even when I look to my relationships, I always felt like I had to be in charge.

Another interesting topic within masculine and feminine energy, especially in relationships, is polarity. Your leading energy reflects your inner nature and values. There are men who have feminine leading energy and women who have masculine leading energy. Understanding your leading energy is necessary to being in flow. In relationships, romantic or otherwise, tension is sometimes caused when both parties are in the same energy which causes an energy clash.

You may both be trying to be more masculine in a situation or both in the feminine, which can be divine at the time but not if you are looking to take action on something. This can then lead to you pushing each other away. But when you are more aware of your behaviours, you can heal yourself from the inside out and have a positive impact on your relationship.

I met Mark only 10 months after my husband left me. I was definitely not looking for a relationship. I was enjoying life, well I thought I was anyway. I was working crazy hours, out partying in the evenings and then on dates in between. It was keeping life interesting, that's for sure. Then one Sunday evening whilst I was browsing the dating site, a message popped up from Mark. It was quite a long message and I nearly didn't reply as not only did he have the same name as my ex-husband, he also had a four-year-old son.

I was definitely not ready to be a stepmum. We chatted on the phone in the evening. I had learnt my lessons from previous dates and knew that emails never guaranteed you'd click in real life. We definitely did and four hours later, at 2am, we finished chatting. We had so much in common, it actually freaked me out a bit. We ended up meeting up for a drink on the Monday and I remember being so attracted to him, my whole body was pulsating. I remember looking at his lips in the pub and thinking… ooh I bet he is a nice kisser. We got kicked out the first pub as it was closing early and quickly drove to another pub so we could carry on chatting.

As we said our goodbyes, my whole body was saying "take him home with you" but I told myself it would be way too naughty so we did a kiss on the cheek and headed back to our cars. It was at that point all this went through my mind: "I like him, his lips look so kissable. I am not going to waste my time if he can't kiss". This was so important for me after so many disastrous dates and yukky kisses, so I walked back from my car and the words blurted out of my mouth – "shall we have a kiss?". His eyes nearly popped out of his head with my forwardness!

We've always said we acted out the Craig David Song, 7 Days – *Monday, took her for a drink on Tuesday, we were making love by Wednesday and on Thursday, Friday, Saturday, we chilled on Sunday*! I always got told you had to wait until the third date, so felt quite proud of myself!

I liked him a lot and could feel myself falling for him but I wouldn't let myself show it.. Plus, I had booked a trip to Thailand and was off two weeks later. I made it very clear, I was going to Thailand single. I wanted to feel free and connect to my travelling days again and I didn't have space for a relationship; it was not on my agenda!

Dance with your masculine & feminine energy

Looking back, I was quite direct with Mark about it too. Mark even took me to the airport and saw me off. Maybe he knew something I didn't?

I had a wild time in Thailand, played and partied hard and did everything I thought I wanted, but it left me feeling rubbish. What was I playing at? I was so wrapped up in fear of being hurt and this was so soon after my marriage ended, I kept telling myself no, you can't do this, no. it's not right, no, no, no.

The first few years of our relationship, I was so guarded. I would never let him in and was always trying to sabotage what was there. I kept telling myself he wasn't right for me because he never liked football and he was too nice! Eventually, three years later, I bit the bullet and moved in with him, whilst renting out my house for security, in case we never made it. Honestly, I don't think until my awakening a few years ago, I was really connected to who I was. We both were in our masculine energy, with me dipping in and out of the wounded feminine energy, that we never connected in the way we have now. When I say It's been a whirlwind for us a couple, that's an understatement and I'll tell you more later in the book.

So let's explore the masculine and feminine energies in you. How do they play out in your life and how can you work with them?

Connection Exercises:

1) What characteristics do you recognise in you?

- Take a moment with yourself now. Close your eyes,

take a few breaths and bring yourself into this moment.

- Take a look back at the wounded and divine aspects of masculine and feminine energy. Do you recognise any of these in yourself? Spend some time making some notes in your journal about how they play out in your world.
- Using the five steps of EAM. Work through the list and sway on each of them, for example "I am controlling", and if you are a Yes (forwards), you can check to see whether you have any resistance, and release. Then align yourself to any of the characteristics you would love to embody.

2) Let's dial up your masculine and feminine energy

Here are some ideas for dialling up your masculine and feminine energy and something you can factor in when you want to move more into one of these energies.

Stepping into your feminine

- Get moving - whether it's going for a walk in a forest, stretching out in a yoga class, or dancing in your underwear to your favourite music in your bedroom, your feminine energy will always be activated by movement.
- Go knickerless for the day - go on, try it and feel the magic!
- Self-pleasure - Is this something you do regularly? Make a date with yourself this week.

- Spend time with the sisterhood - book a date with your girlfriends.
- Create something beautiful - when was the last time you did something creative? Pencil in some time and get those creative juices flowing.
- Practice receiving love - make an intention to fully receive today; every compliment you receive, say thank you and try and feel it in your heart

Dialling up your masculine energy

- Step into your confidence - this may not be something that is natural to you, but give it a go and start with asking for what you want - look at the reaction you get from those around you.
- Do things outside your comfort zone - is there something you have been want to do for ages? Can you take that step today?
- Set Intentions and stick to them - if this is something that doesn't come naturally, give it a go and start with a small intention until you feel more confident
- Speak up – has something been bugging you but you wouldn't dare say - speak up and see how it feels.

PUTTING YOU FIRST

I don’t have time for myself is one of the biggest excuses I hear from my clients, but what I always say back is – It’s not you don’t have time, it’s because you don’t make the time.

We all have the same amount of time in a day, 24 hours, and you have a choice of how you spend your time. It really is that simple. For me, my time is so precious, so whatever I do now, has to be something I enjoy doing or I don't do it. I live my life by this mantra and it has made a big impact on my energy levels and positive mindset. You shouldn't do anything you don't want to do.

Are you someone who moans about doing so much for others and never having time for yourself? If this is the case, why are you doing it?

If your default is to over give, this may feel like a challenge for you because if it’s what you have always done, you don’t know any other way. One of the most common reasons for this is, you don’t think you are worth spending time on and everything else is more important than you. If you are not consciously, aware you can always check in with EAM. I want you to know, my darling, the first step is recognising it; then you can start exploring what life would look like when you do. Even if it feels out of reach at the moment, keep focussing on it and every day, make baby steps towards it. I have included a connection exercise at the end of this chapter for you to explore this and make some plans for your ideal week.

Consent and Boundaries

Putting boundaries in place around your time is one way you can get more time for yourself. Until I discovered the world of Tantra massage, I didn't even know consent and boundaries was something to be aware of. Having an understanding of these has enabled me to step more into my truth about what I desire and how I communicate with others. How can I get what I want whilst feeling safe and free enough to explore the edges of my experience? This isn't just about physical boundaries though and you can apply this to all areas of your life.

The dictionary definition of consent and boundaries are:

Personal boundaries are limits or guidelines we set to others around how they behave and interact with us.

Consent - permission for something to happen or agreement to do something.

Consent and boundaries go hand in hand, because having someone's permission for something to happen, or agreement to do something, is crucial.

I always put myself first so I am the best version of me

When you set boundaries, you can consent from a place of empowerment. What is it that you want? What are you happy with? As with everything that I teach, it all starts with YOU.

When I work with clients, especially in tantric massage, boundaries and consent are always discussed up front. I ask them questions like: How do they feel about receiving touch? Where would they like to be touched and what is ok and what isn't? We also have various check ins throughout the experience for them to tune in to how they feel and whether they consent to continue. I explore consent with touch later in the book.

Are you willing to set boundaries and, most importantly, stick to them?

I know from my journey, it also came down to self-love. The more I loved who I was, the more aware I became around my time, thoughts and emotions, and setting boundaries became easier. It transformed everything, because before that, I had no boundaries. Boundaries are learnt behaviour and if your boundaries were violated in any way, especially as a child, you may not know what they mean. In my adult life, I would work all the hours, give all of myself to everything and everyone and it became a way of life. I would never tell someone if they took advantage of my time or if I didn't want to do something. I was scared they would stop liking me or it would reflect badly on me in some way.

There are many types of boundaries but let's explore a few here:

Emotional - Are you able to separate your own emotions to others? Can you take responsibility for your emotions? Healthy boundaries prevent you from giving advice, blaming or accepting blame. They protect you from feeling guilty for someone else's negative feelings or problems and taking others' comments personally.

Mental - This applies to your thoughts, values, and opinions. Do you know what you believe, and can you hold on to your opinions? Can you listen with an open mind to someone else's opinion without becoming rigid? If you become highly emotional, argumentative or defensive, you may have weak emotional boundaries

Material - Do you give away or lend money, cars, clothes, possessions easily and does it feel good when you do?

Physical - Do you have a boundary over your physical space, the way others interact with you? Are you happy to receive hugs, kisses? How do you feel being around others naked?

Spiritual – These boundaries relate to your beliefs and experiences in connection with God or a higher power and spirit.

Sexual – These protect your comfort level with sexual touch and activity – where do you like to be touched, when, and with whom? What's ok when it comes to sexual interaction with someone and what's not ok? And are you able to communicate these?

Time – Do you value your time or do you keep yourself so busy to the point of exhaustion? Do you let your clients/colleagues book in when you have already planned something for yourself? Do you work when you had plans to have a night doing something fun?

What lights you up?

Boundaries give you power. They allow you to completely own your way of being, across all areas of your life, but they take practice - first to know what they are, then to set them, communicate them to others and stick to them. It's important to note here, boundaries can change moment to moment. Something that may have felt ok once can change to not feeling ok. Boundaries are also about speaking up and communicating when it changes.

I've learnt so much about boundaries over the last four years whilst exploring my sexuality. I found the most amazing place, Osho Leela, a personal development space that runs workshops and retreats. I have attended the sexuality festivals there over the last two years. Throughout the week at the workshops we always had conversations up front about what our boundaries were. I think for most of my life, my default was to say I didn't have any and I thought at the time meant I was being free in myself. It has been so powerful to set boundaries and make decisions with touch and exploring my sexuality, and has been fundamental in me feeling safe. There is so much expansion to be experienced when you stick to those, although I have definitely made some mistakes along the way and learnt what happens when you get drunk on love.

I learnt although they can change from moment to moment, it's best they are set when you are 'sober'. This made so much sense, although at the festivals, we were always sober as they are conscious sexuality festivals, which means no alcohol or drugs. You can absolutely get carried away in the moment so it's best they are set when you are 'sober' so you don't decide to ignore them and push the boundary up a level as this can leave you feeling violated in some way.

The latest boundary I have been exploring is in the spiritual world. This is relatively new to me. I had no idea you could have boundaries with spirit but the truth is, you can put them in place across everything.

I have been on such a huge journey with death during my awakening. I used to be so scared of dying after losing so many people I love in tragic circumstances. A few years ago, I started working in a dementia home. I became so close to death and had the most beautiful moments with my clients as they transitioned. One day, I watched as my client's spirit leave her body. I was on my own but I remember feeling so privileged to have witness something so beautiful in someone I had gotten to know so well over the years. These experiences healed my fear of death and without intention, I have now started to receive lots of downloads from spirits.

This has come in so many ways; lots of messages for others from their loved ones and recently, I had an experience last year after I lost a friend and they transitioned through me as they left this world. I felt so overwhelmed and for a few days didn't realise what was happening. I knew I felt very strange and I was definitely in my own energy and then one day, after being in bed for days, he left me with a thank you. I spoke to some of my medium friends afterwards, they explained I could tell spirit if it felt too much and I wasn't in a space to help them right now. This felt amazing and as this is all so new to me, it made me feel a lot better. I now put them in place when I need too.

Boundaries are a big topic and maybe like me, you have never had any, but it doesn't mean you can't start to put them in place now. So let's explore how you spend your time to see whether you can make more time for you, and also explore what boundaries you already have and others you could put in place.

Connection Exercises:

1) What do you LOVE about your day to day and what would you like to change?

Take a moment now to close your eyes and drop yourself into a typical week, go through your day and notice how it feels in your body when you think of all the things you do:

- Do you have things you dislike doing?
- Why don't you like them?
- Does it stop you doing something else you would rather be doing?
- Have you stopped doing something you love because you are so busy?
- What is stopping you from not doing it anymore?

Now sit and journal on these and make note of the things you are saying to yourself - are these thoughts in alignment with you?

You can then use the five steps of EAM to transform these thoughts and bring in all the delicious things you would love to be doing.

Then embody this. Spend some time imagining your week looking exactly how you'd like it and notice how it feels in your body. You can come back to this anytime you desire.

2) Let's explore your boundaries

In this exercise, I would like you to spend some time exploring the following questions:

- Do I have boundaries in place across any areas of my life?
- Looking through the types of boundaries I've explained, where would you like to put boundaries in place?
- What stops you? Make note of any thoughts or emotions that arise when you do.
- What one boundary can you practice putting in place in your life for yourself?

I know from my journey, having firm boundaries takes time. The more you practice upholding these for yourself, the more you will learn and the more engrained they will become.

THE POWER OF SEXUAL ENERGY

This is probably the chapter I am most excited you've got to. Everything I have shared with you already is an important foundation in exploring the power of sexual energy and I know you had to be ready to even go here. Does talking about sex feel awkward to you or is it something you have always loved but never daren't tell a soul?

When it was awakened in me, I did not know what to do with it. I now know it's great to be sexually alive and to embrace all the pleasure in me. I am going to teach you how to tap into sexual energy. When you do, it's a way of life and it impacts everything.

So what is sexual energy and why is it so powerful?

Before I go on and explain more of what happened when I woke up to it, let me explain what sexual energy is.

Sexual energy is your creative life force energy. It is so powerful that it can create life; it's what brought you into this world. If you think about the vibration of energy, sexual energy is not only high in vibration, it's expansive too and this deep connection has the power for you to birth anything in this world. This can include physical manifestations or the confidence for you to stand in your truth.

It is so much more than sex. Of course having sex alone or with another can connect you to the energy but you can also connect to it fully clothed without even touching yourself.

Connecting to my sexual energy has hands down transformed my life.

When I connected to this powerful energetic force within me, I was able to heal from my past, from the part of myself I hid, and it connected me more deeply into life. It's a huge topic and there is so much growth and expansion to be explored here. I'm going to be explaining in this chapter, how you can start the conversation with this part of you and how you can start to activate this energy even if it's something you feel is not part of your life right now.

Before I do, I would love you to take a moment now and take a breath to check in with yourself:

- How does it feel to be talking about sexual energy?
- Is it something that feels good or does something come up in you?

Take a few breaths here and however you are feeling, it's ok. Accept it.

Sexual energy is life energy

But first, let me tell you a little more about the moment this surge of sexual energy began to awaken in me. It totally freaked me out. It came to me when I was meditating, I mean you couldn't get a quieter space to make an impact.

I didn't understand why I had gone from being someone that was 'normal' to being here, where I was having explicit dreams about fucking everyone in sight. I was so wild in my dreams. I quite enjoyed what I was seeing at times but I was also full of so much shame - I couldn't be that woman?! It made me feel so ashamed to be having these thoughts at all.

The first thing I did was try and squash it down; it felt too much. I had never felt anything like it before. I was in a relationship and it felt so disruptive. My god, I did my best to block it out at first. I didn't dare share it with Mark, I felt so guilty for what I was seeing and feeling.

Not long after that, I made the decision to invest in myself for the first time and join The Energy Alignment Method® ten-month collective programme. It was a big deal and another leap of faith for me. I had always invested in myself to help others, but never for my own self development. I had no idea what I was signing up for, I just knew it was something I needed to do.

On the first weekend, we did a vision meditation and at the end of the vision, everyone was frantically writing down what they saw. I was annoyed, as I said I saw nothing - well I saw a little girl lost in the woods and trying to find her way… I had no idea what it meant.

The truth is, I had never connected to the truth of who I was. I always felt like two people; one side of me was Kerry the Mum, holistic and spending my time doing lots for others, but... I also had this wild sexual goddess side that had always been there in the background and was starting to come out again. I had spent so much of my life squashing this part of me down and now it wanted to be listened to.

I remember doing a VIP day with Yvette Taylor. It was the first time I had shared what had been going on and it felt so refreshing to say it out loud and to someone that I felt so safe with. In the session, we explored at what age in my life I started to connect to my sexual energy and also when I started to disconnect from this part of me. I was five. This was such a shock to me and I didn't understand how that could be.

I lost my virginity when I was 15. I was on holiday in Tenerife with my friends, Joanne and Helen. I couldn't believe my mum let me go. I remember being so excited; two weeks in the sunshine, dancing and drinking with my friends! A group of lads we knew were out there too, including a lad I'd been seeing and I was looking forward to seeing him again. I couldn't wait to be alone with him and as soon as we got together, I knew it was time. I'd heard so many horror stories about people's firsts but I had a great time. I remember us doing lots of different positions and I thought it was pretty good for my first time. As we finished, I was mortified to see blood on the sheets and I remembering panicking his friends would see and know I was a virgin. It was a big deal I'd lost my virginity and when I got back to my apartment and told the girls, they were cracking up, singing 'Kerry is no longer a Virgin.' I never forget calling my mum from a payphone later that day and Helen shouting out 'Kerry has lost her virginity'. Needless to say when I got home, my mum sat down and had "the chat" with me.

I was always quite open about sex and at the time I had the VIP day, had no reason to think I'd had any trauma linked to sex.

Across the next few months, I started to get flashbacks from times in my life when I was taken advantage off. I had never told a soul about any of this and it had been suppressed in my memory all these years. I had kept myself so busy all my life; other people were my focus, I worked hard, played hard, I never stopped... because when I did, I felt uncomfortable.

I have so many memories now going back to when I was five. For most of them, I had no idea it was abuse and although I was told to be quiet and not tell anyone, I thought it was how men showed love. This played out so much in my life and I found myself in so many situations where I was powerless and felt I had no choice but to be brave.

One of the memories that came back so clearly in my mind was when I went on a weekend away with the local Youth Club. It was an adventure weekend with potholing and outdoor activities. I remember one of the leaders from the centre showing me a lot of attention and all of my friends giggling saying he fancied me. I was only about 8 at the time and remember feeling embarrassed and not knowing what to do. He seemed to be there a lot and I can still see him smiling at me, which I suppose is called grooming now. It gives me the shudders thinking about it as I had no idea at the time. Later on, he came over to chat to me and asked me to come to the TV room when everyone was in bed as he had something he wanted to show me. He was quite persistent and said I wasn't allowed to tell anyone about it. I did what he told me and we sat there watching TV and I remember the moment he put his arms around me, I froze. He then assaulted me. He told me to be quiet, that I was beautiful and made me touch him and give him a blow job. It wasn't aggressive but I was scared and he told me I wasn't allowed to tell anyone or we would both get in trouble. So I didn't. As I'm writing this, I'm crying for my little 8-year-old self who was so scared and thought this was how it was. I have never said all this out loud. The morning afterwards, I couldn't wait to see him. I thought he liked me. He couldn't even look at me. I felt so ashamed. We left to go home and it was another secret I internalised for my whole life, until now.

A few months later, the memories were coming thick and fast and I remembered the night I was raped. It came in lots of sketchy memories and at this point, I was totally questioning myself whether any of this was true. I was so overwhelmed. How could I have forgot about all of this for over 30 years? When the memory came up, it took me so long to accept it happened and I was so scared to share this but also knew I had to. It was part of me and accepting it was my truth. I never told anyone as I thought no one would believe me, and I blamed myself. I led him on... I must have given the impression it was ok... I didn't say no loud enough... so many things meant I had to bury it. I was ashamed with myself that it had happened and I never told anyone at the time. This has been such a profound part of my journey. Out of all the abuse I'd experienced in my life, when this happened, I knew it was wrong. I knew this was not ok but I had no power in me, in my own self-belief and self-worth, to do anything about it. I don't even remember letting myself feel any of the trauma. I told myself no, I couldn't go there, and I blamed myself.

Breathe, give yourself space to feel what's alive in you

Looking back, I realise for most of my life, sex was just a function for me. I was quite wild in my university days but I always felt so dirty when I let myself go and had laid there so many times letting men do what they wanted to me. I wasn't connected to the moment, to what I wanted, and even though I had slept with a lot of men in my past, I experienced my first orgasm when I was married. I didn't even realise my pleasure was even a thing. Everything makes so much sense now and I know it all comes back to how disconnected I had become with myself.

My journey with EAM began the journey of connecting to the person I was underneath all the numbness, to connect to everything I felt about myself and to become aware of all the feelings I had around shame and self-worth. I now know that the little girl in the woods that day was me. I had been lost in my childhood all my adult life without knowing it at all. I had protected myself to the point of being numb and never allowed myself to receive love, especially from myself.

This acknowledgement, through the awakening of my sexual energy, started the journey to heal myself. One of my friends recommended I go and see a Tantra massage practitioner to work on the trauma I had remembered, and to learn to love myself again. I had never heard of Tantra before and although nervous, I knew I had to book a session. I found someone who did Tantra sessions in London and before I knew it, an Airbnb was booked for my four-hour experience. I was so scared but I knew it was a pivotal moment in my life. I knew I had to do it.

When I arrived, the studio flat was alight with beautiful candles and smelt gorgeous, there were soft blankets and it looked like the perfect setting for the amazing sensual experience that followed. The session started with a detailed chat. We talked about why I was there, what were my intentions for the sessions and most importantly, how I was feeling and what were my boundaries for the session. I then had a lovely warm shower and changed into my sarong and we started with some non-touch connection exercises which included eye gazing and breath work, followed by a number of full body massages including breast and yoni massage (Sanskrit name for the womb).

At each stage, I was asked did I give permission for this area to be touched. It was a two-way communication the entire time, with me communicating how I felt throughout the experience. I had never experienced anything like this before and although it was sensual, I was completely in the role of the receiver, there was no obligation for me to give back, so I could allow myself to completely surrender to receiving love.

I don't think I had ever received love with ease and here I was, embracing all of me, all of my body. I physically released the trauma I experienced all those years ago. I screamed, I cried and I let go. It was mind-blowing. I knew from that day, I had found my path and this experience led me to then go on and train as a Tantra Massage Practitioner as I had this inner feeling that I was here to show others the way too - how they could fully surrender and let go. I spent the next three years continuing the journey, releasing more trauma and exploring my mind, body and sexuality.

This is part of my self-care now and I honestly think every being on this planet should experience Tantra Massage on a regular basis. It's incredible and I feel so blessed to have found it at that stage in my journey and for it still to be such a huge part of my world today.

I share all this with you because I want you to know, I had no idea I was so disconnected, that I even had trauma or that I hadn't known myself. This energy was so powerful and so alive in me that it was screaming at me to listen and has now been a huge part in setting me free.

So how do you activate sexual energy in you?

For some people, activating sexual energy feels easy and for others it can feel like something far removed from their everyday reality. The response I get most when I ask how someone activates sexual energy in themselves is through having sex or self-pleasuring. There are lots of ways you can activate it in you, on command, and use it for whatever you desire. I wake mine up all the time. I think of it as an energetic boost and I love the aliveness I feel in me when I do.

Having a healthy relationship with sex is vital to harness the power that is there to be experienced. If you are someone that is used to shutting it down or has some shame around it, this will cause resistance in the body and energy won't flow, it won't have activated to its full expansion. Wherever you are in the journey, there is always more magic to be experienced. That's what excites me about sharing this magic with the world.

But before we go into some of the exercises, let's have another check in - How is this feeling for you? If you feel like something is coming up for you, take a breath. If you need to create some space for you to integrate any of this within yourself, take it. This whole journey is about listening to YOU. There is no need to rush anything; it's a journey, not a race.

If you feel ready to start exploring this, let's get started with some connection exercises to understand your relationship with sexual energy and start the journey to activating it in your beautiful being:

Connection Exercises:

1) What's your relationship with sexual energy?

Spend a few moments now and think back to your relationship with sexual energy over the years:

- Was sex discussed when you were growing up? What do you remember?
- Do you remember when you first discovered sex/sexual energy?
- Is it something you connect with?
- Does it feel comfortable? If not, do you know why?

2) Activate your Sexual energy

This is a great exercise to activate and move sexual energy throughout the body. It's also a great way to release tension in your pelvis and connect to your sensual self. Throughout the exercise, remember to breathe, allow your body to move how it wants too and let yourself make any sounds that feels natural.

Always remember BREATH, SOUND, MOVEMENT - this is key in tantric practices as it gets the energy moving and enables it to flow through your body.

I feel the aliveness within me

If throughout this practice, you don't feel like anything is happening, know it takes time and although you may not be feeling it in your mind or in your body, this activation is moving energy and it may take more practice for you to feel embodied with it.

On the flipside, you may feel lots. My invitation is for you to let the emotions flow, give yourself permission to feel everything that arises as it's very much part of the processing of awakening you.

- Start by standing up and placing your feet hip width apart.
- Start gently rocking your pelvis back and forth - As your hips go forward, I want you to squeeze in your pelvic floor muscles and as you go back you push out – continue to do it until it feels natural and you get into a rhythm.
- See how it feels to move your hips in a circular motion and carry this on until you feel yourself getting into a rhythm.
- Acknowledge how this is feeling . Are you aware of anything happening in your body? What can you feel?
- Start to get the rest of your body involved – how does it feel to be moving the pelvis in this way?
- If it feels good, start caressing your body and start to move the energy upwards from your pelvis to your heart and to your head out to your arms.
- You could do this for hours but I would love you to do it for at least 10 minutes.
- When you do eventually stop, take a moment with yourself. Close your eyes and feel the energy within

you and spend some time being present with how this feels for you.

Once you have spent some moments in silence, sit down comfortably and take a few deep breaths into your body and connect with what you had written in the previous exercise about Sexual Energy. Grab your journal and give the following questions some thought:

- How did it feel?
- Did you notice anything happening in your body when you wrote about your relationship?
- How did the sexual energy activation feel? Breathe all of the awareness in.
- If you felt nothing, note it down too.

PUSSY POWER

I used to hate the word Pussy, it repulsed me. I thought it was so rude and was definitely not an area of my body I thought was powerful. When I read the book *Pussy – A Reclamation, by Regena Thomashauer*, it totally changed my opinion of the word and I got my head around giving mine a name and what I felt about my own and how I referred to her.

It depends on my mood what I call her but what I now acknowledge is she is a beautifully sacred part of me. Sometimes I call her pussy, my yoni or vulva, and you'll notice I refer to all of these in the book. With my little one, it's called a moo moo (not sure where I got that one!). Do you have a name for yours?

I had no idea how much power there was to be reclaimed in this beautiful part of my body. I had never given her any consideration, any respect, I used to say such awful things about her. Not only did I think she looked disgusting, I was also so numb that it was an area I had never touched or acknowledged.

Is your pussy asleep?

As I started exploring my sexuality, I heard so many stories of self-pleasure journeys. Mine only started three years ago and, apart from one time where I explored her in the bath and was left riddled with shame, I ignored her my entire life.

I know this is common and so many women feel the same way. They ignore her and say horrible things and what happens then? The pussy doesn't awaken, she doesn't want to play, she loses the desire to feel pleasure and can almost go dormant and go to sleep. She can then become numb and that's what happened to me.

Pussy power is such a hugely untapped resource for women and there are so many ways we can connect with her. I hope reading this inspires you to explore her power, even if this feels like an edge for you. There is no end to the depth of connection here; the more you connect, the deeper you will go. But it's not a race, think of it as a start of a new relationship, an exploration that will grow in time.

You might be starting to feel something in your pussy now as you read this - she absolutely loves being talked about and loves attention. I always remember the reference in the book Pussy, about the energy being like a lamp. The more you connect, the more she wakes up and the brighter she shines but the moment you start to ignore her and stop paying her attention, she switches off. She does not like to be ignored and you may find it takes some time for you to start your relationship with her. She may need some persuasion to turn her light on, especially if it's been a while since you have said hello.

Pussy power can be used for EVERYTHING! It's life energy, helps you give birth to new ideas, connects you to your creativity, to joy, to pleasure and has the ability to transform your energy in an instant.

I can honestly say, hand on heart, connecting to pussy power has transformed my life, my business, everything. From a place of disgust three years ago, it's now my go to energy on a daily basis. A warning though, she can be extremely distracting once she has woken up.

Before I go on to explain how you can connect to this power, let me give you a little anatomy lesson on the outer parts of the pussy (the vulva). I wish someone had given me this. I had no idea what was down there. Let alone what all the bits were called!

Let me start by telling you that everyone's pussy look's different but we all have the same things. One of the biggest hang ups I had about my pussy was how it looked. The look of mine repulsed me as I thought mine was so different to anyone else's. In films, they always look so polished and look the same, so I thought mine was abnormal!

The beautiful diagram was drawn by my gorgeous friend, Jennifer. I loved her representation of the vulva and it may help you in your exploration.

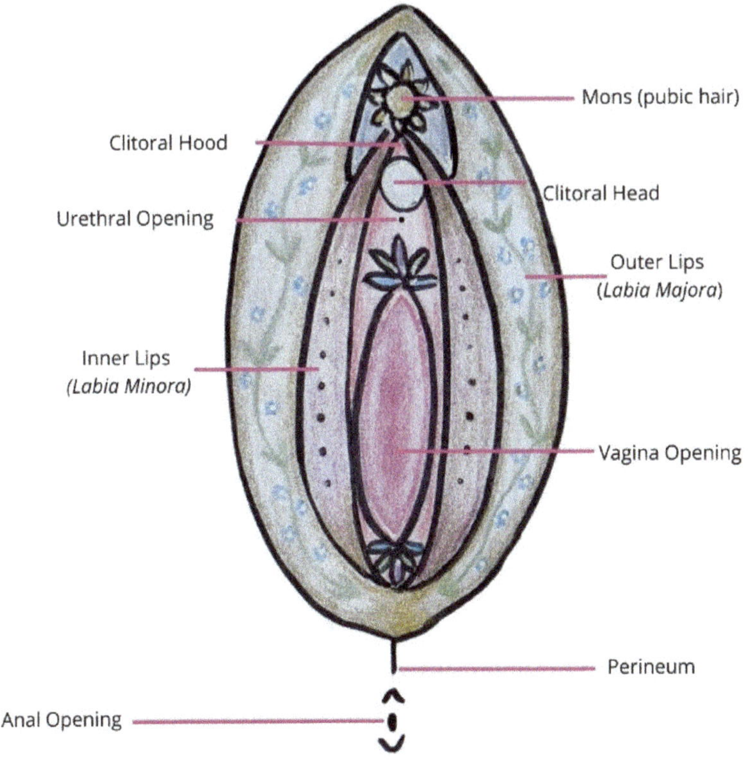

In the book, Women's Anatomy of Arousal, I love how Sheri Winston describes the female genitalia as having three concentric zones – The Yard, The Porch and Inner Sanctum - '*Imagine a lush garden surrounding an inviting portico that leads into a beautiful temple*':

The Yard are the outer areas you can see and include the mons (mound of Venus as it's sometimes referred) which is a pad of fatty tissue that is covered in pubic hair, although with the current craze in Hollywood wax, may be hairless. It can be a super sensitive area but can also be numb. The outer lips are the larger of the two and come in all shapes and sizes;

sometimes they can be plump or sometimes thinner and slender. They can also change colour and size depending on the level of arousal.

As you venture in a little, you'll arrive at the *porch*. This includes the inner labia; you may need to spread the outer lips out so they reveal themselves. The clitoral hood can vary in size and the clitoris is sometimes hidden by the hood or peeping outside of it. The Clitoris, complete with its 8000 nerve endings, is a lot bigger than you may expect. Its legs extend down underneath the labia adding to the depth of arousal this beautiful part of you can experience. It also includes the areas that surround the vaginal openings - the anus and the urethra (where you pee from).

Leading to the *Inner Sanctum,* which is the Vagina and anal canal – the most scared areas. In between these is a smooth area of the skin, the Perineum. It has fewer nerve endings than the rest of the genitalia but as it's an area that is often cut during childbirth, it can be extremely sensitive or numb and there may be scaring in the area. I find massage of the perineum extremely comforting and grounding.

Your Pussy is uniquely beautiful and can be explored and touched in different ways. The beauty is in the exploration of yourself and getting to know yours.

Do you remember the time when you first connected to your pussy or even noticed she was there? It was only a few years ago I started this exploration and at the beginning, I had no idea. It all felt so alien to me. So if the thought of this feels really uncomfortable, know there is no right or wrong here. Being here may be marking the beginning of the journey for you and that's perfect.

The relationship with our pussy can be dependent on so many factors and similar to the discovery of sexual energy, can be impacted by your childhood and what you were told growing up.

These and many more things will all have an impact on how you connect with her and if you are out of alignment and have resistant thoughts, beliefs and emotions about the connection to your pussy, this will all be impacting on the depth of that connection. When connected, you have the ability to feel her warmth; she will nourish you and give you an energy boost and help connect you to your desires, to pleasure and to all life has to offer you.

Trauma in the pussy

It is important to acknowledge here if there is any pain or numbness or feelings of disconnection in your pussy, it can be because of tension and trauma experienced in this area.

Have you ever remembered a time when you've felt pain in this area? This could be from experiencing sexual trauma in your life by another, inserting a tampon, through childbirth or when you've had sex and it's hurt but you've carried on anyway. You can also feel pain here when you've lost someone special in your life or when someone close to you has been hurt. She can be impacted by anything that happens in life and even if it's something that you have never consciously acknowledged, it may be stored within your physical body.

When your pussy is in pain, she is trying to get your attention, but it's an area that is often ignored. The pussy talks to you and when you start to connect with her, she will be awakened and in communication with you all the time. Have a think of a moment when you have been attracted to someone – have you ever felt your pussy twinge and pulsate?

This can also happen when you are watching a movie and there's a really romantic sex scene and your pussy responds with a feeling like – ooh, yes please. I know when my pussy is engaged, it feels like there is a furnace between my legs; she is so warm and alive, it feels quite comforting. Right now, as I am writing about her, she has woken her up. She likes to have attention and when she gets it, she will gift you with pleasure.

This can be in various forms – warmth, tingling, pulsating. It's a reminder she is there and she is awake. If you are nervously laughing, know the more you accept the power she has, the more you will start to acknowledge and experience with her. She also lets you know when she isn't happy too; my pussy draws backwards when she is a no. Like with the EAM Sway, the pussy can help you to make decisions. She absolutely knows what she wants when she is listened to. You can explore what a yes and a no feel like in the connection exercises.

When I connected to the trauma in my pussy, I followed the same pattern of trying to push it down. When I first recognised the disconnect, I had started seeing a sex therapist to try and understand why sexual energy had become so alive in me and why I couldn't stop thinking about sex all the time. It was all head energy though. I felt like I had something wrong that needed fixing. We explored the relationship I had with my body. I always held a part of my belly whenever I wanted to be comforted, until then, I hadn't taken any time to acknowledge it. Just below my belly button was this ring of warmth and it felt so safe.

What is your pussy saying to you?

What I hadn't realised until then that beneath the warmth, the area of the pelvis and the pussy was ice cold, completely and utterly numb. The ring around my belly was protecting me, it was a place of safety for me and something I had created when I decided I would not let myself feel the pain in that area. I remember us doing a beautiful ritual where we told the ring of protection I was ready to feel, ready to see what was beneath it. I cried my eyes out when we cut the energetic chords connected to it and gave it permission to leave. I remember afterwards feeling so empty, like I had lost a big part of who I was. It was the strangest feeling and it took me some time to accept this empty feeling was me feeling something I hadn't felt before. I was started to bring life to an area of my body I'd numbed for so long.

When I trained in Tantric massage, it set me on a journey to embody everything I was feeling and I became closer to understanding why I had created this protection around myself in the first place and although I had worked on the thoughts and the beliefs I had around the night I was raped, there was more to be acknowledged

Over two and a half years ago, I was at back in Bristol at the Tantra Massage Training school, but this time, wasn't learning. I was offering my body for the practice so others could learn how to give Tantric massage. I always found these weekends so magical. To actually learn this beautiful sacred massage on a real person, was phenomenal and I learnt so much. This was the second time I had volunteered as a Shakti bunny (a name we gave to those who volunteered) and each time, I was blown away by the power of not only giving my body in service for those that were learning, but also for what I let go each time I received one. When I arrived in Bristol the night before, I could feel loads of emotions starting to rise to the surface. They came out of nowhere, so I sat down and I wrote out what I was feeling and even I was shocked when I put it into words:

I feel like I don't want anyone to touch me.

I'm feeling unsafe.

I feel like I'm unable to hold any boundaries and that I can be overpowered easily by others.

I feel vulnerable.

I don't feel in my power.

I feel like I've slipped into my younger self and don't want to put myself in any bad situations.

But there's a part of me that wants it too.

I want to be made to feel used.

That's a feeling that I was always used to.

I recognise that pain.

But deep down it scares me.

I don't like being in this place, I want my power back again.

This was me in my complete raw state. I wasn't in my 39-year-old body, I was 17 again, although at the time, I had no idea what was happening. That night, I did nothing else but sleep and sit with the words I had expressed on paper.

I woke up early and went out for my run. I always did this before a workshop to clear my mind. As soon as I set off, the tears started and I couldn't stop crying. I spoke with a couple of friends that morning. I wanted to be heard and explain how I was feeling and it was so comforting. I knew I had the tools to work on this but wanted someone to hold my hand.

I called one of my amazing friends and fellow EAM mentors, Kerry-Ann, and in no time at all, we cleared an imprint on my energy from when I was raped. Although I had worked on this before, this was different. I had a connection with the person that did it and I needed to set him free.

I have never spoken about him and how I felt. The truth is, he was someone I admired and looked up to. I think that's why I never told anyone, I was so shocked he actually did it. I know I said no, and my no wasn't heard. I have never felt anger towards him; I have always felt so sad he had done this to me. I remember looking at him afterwards and he couldn't even look at me. I felt disgusting, I felt ashamed and I felt used. I remember so clearly pulling up my ripped tights and walking straight into one of my friends who asked if I was ok. I said yeah. I remember looking into her eyes and I was speechless. I was in so much shock, I never told anyone and tried to forget about it. I blamed myself. I thought it was my fault.

So that day in Bristol, after I cleared the imprint, I arrived at the course. I felt back in my power again but I felt so nervous and was fearful of the afternoon yoni massage practice and who I was going to work with. As this was a part of a teaching piece, I stayed connected with the person I was working with, giving feedback as he massaged me and then, when it became painful, I asked for the treatment to stop and asked to be wrapped in a blanket and laid there.

I felt a rush of panic come over me. I couldn't breathe and I felt suffocated. I jumped up, wrapped a sarong around me and went to leave the room. I wanted to escape and run away. At that moment, some people had arrived outside the room on their way to the upstairs area. I knew I couldn't leave then, so I lay on the floor and cried. All I kept thinking was about that night. I didn't ask for any of this, I said no and he never stopped.

All the emotions of the things I was feeling then were coming out: I screamed No, I said No, why did you do this to me? I was sobbing and my whole body was shaking. I now know this was my body releasing the trauma and I remember the first time this happened, desperately trying to stop it. I felt like it was taking over my entire body, it was overwhelming and I wanted it to stop. I was so scared and had no idea this was the energy moving through me.

One of the assistants was with me. She asked me what I needed. I felt her there and I asked her to tell me I was safe and hold my hand. Having her there helped me release some more. I covered myself in a blanket as I felt so ashamed of myself and didn't want anyone to see me. How could I have kept this inside me for so long and still have so much trauma left inside my body? I was experiencing all the emotions I felt back then but had never expressed.

Afterwards, which felt like forever, I stop shaking and dropped into stillness and my energy came back to the room. I realised where I was. I felt so embarrassed and I was in so much shock. I went from feeling 'ok' to having this out of body experience. My god, I knew this work was powerful but it amazed me how much every single time I let go. I remember at the end of the workshop, we all sat in circle and we shared three words. I don't remember the exact words but I remember sharing that I was so ashamed of the way I was feeling and what had just happened.

Later in the evening, I left for my three hours' home. I always loved those drives as it helped me integrate before getting back to family life. I remember thinking, how on earth am I going to be able to be interviewed on a radio station tomorrow and resume normal life?

I did though, and instead of pretending I was ok, I spoke my truth. I spoke to Mark about what had happened and went to bed. In the weeks that followed, I spent a lot of time going over it all in my mind and processing what had happened. I did lots of EAM work to clear any feelings of embarrassment and shame and aligned to trusting this was all part of my journey to complete freedom from my past.

It made me realise, we are on an evolving journey and there is no such thing as being fixed. Each time your body let's go, it's always something different, a different angle or perspective released.

I share this part of my journey with you as I want you to know how powerful this work is and how important it is for you to lean in to it all. Although at first it can feel so overwhelming, the other side of letting go is freedom, and that feeling is worth every part of the pain I have experienced in moving it through my body.

So let's start exploring the relationship you have with your pussy…

Connection Exercises:

1) What's the relationship with your pussy?

This is a journaling exercise. I would like you to sit down and have some time for you to think about the relationship you have with your pussy. I would love you to free flow your writing here but I have left some questions below which may help get you started. This may feel quite tough to write about or it may feel easy. Let the words flow and try not to overthink it. If you feel there may be resistance to doing the exercise, you have the wonderful tool of EAM to help release any resistance you may have to getting started and if you feel anything arising in you as you explore these questions.

- When did you first notice her?
- How did your self-pleasure journey begin or has it ever started?
- How was the pussy talked about growing up with parents and friends etc.?
- Was it a place that was considered disgusting or was it something openly talked about?
- Do you remember a time when you were connected to her?
- Do you remember a time when she was in pain and you never listened?
- Do you know how it feels when she is switched on?
- How often do you connect to her?
- What does this practice look like?
- How does it feel?
- Do you say beautiful things to her or do you say nasty things?

2) Having a chat with your pussy

Before you deepen the connection to your pussy, this is a beautiful way to start talking to her and to start the practice of asking and listening to what she has to say. Know, like with all the embodiment exercises I share with you, sometimes they take some time to get the conversation flowing, especially if she has never been connected in this way before.

- Get yourself nice and comfortable, seated or lay down, whatever feels good for you in this moment.
- Close your eyes and take three deep breaths.
- Now draw your attention to your pussy and connect to her
- Practice asking her questions - here are some examples below - and then acknowledge and make any notes of what she says:
- Hello, how are you today?
- Have you missed me?
- Would you like me to communicate with you in this way?
- Would you like to be touched?

3) Pussy Breathing

This has got to be one of my favourite ways to connect to my pussy, to feel and embody her energy. I use this practice often and it only takes a few minutes. If you found the last two exercise a challenge, this may help you to connect with her in a more embodied way and can feel really yummy the more you do it.

- Sit or lie down, whatever feels nourishing for you right now.
- Take a few normal breaths, inhaling through your nose and out through your mouth, dropping into this moment.
- If it feels good, place your hands over your pussy now and cup her.
- Take a deep breath in and focus on squeezing the breath right up into your vagina, squeezing in your pelvic floor muscle and hold.
- Then exhale and let your pussy full relax.
- Do this for a few breaths or set a timer and do it as an active meditation.
- Spend a few moments afterwards acknowledging how it felt for you.

Later on in the book, we will be doing some more exploration of your pussy with touch but know these conversations and connection through breath can go a long way in deepening the connection before you even begin to touch her.

SO WHAT DOES YOUR HEART DESIRE?

When you start to explore to the depths of your soul and awakening your sexual energy, the next step of awakening is connecting to what you desire. What do I want from my life?

Don't worry if your first response is "I have no idea", especially if it's been quite some time since you have even considered asking yourself.

What does desire actually mean to you? Do you know what you desire? Or do you have absolute no idea and don't even think it's accessible right now?

Our desires can sometimes feel so far away, as if they are a luxury and not realistic to achieve. If in the past, there have been times when your dreams have been shattered, you may think it's meaningless to have desires. With so many unfulfilled desires, you may be losing faith and trust they can ever be a reality. Know that everything is possible when you believe you can.

Desire comes from a place of surrender

When you embody your desires, they become a big part of your expansion. Even the dreams you don't think are possible, become your reality. Only then, can you expand the depth of your desire. It's never ending; there is always more you can experience if you keep dreaming and live in an energy of pure abundance, knowing it can all become your reality – if it's what you desire.

Desires guide you to what you most want to manifest. Other words for desire include eagerness, fascination, hunger, lust, thirst, wish. Ooh yummy, try saying the words out loud. Can you feel them in your body? I can!

For me though, it's more than embodiment. It's about surrendering into the divine and trusting all will come to you if it's meant to. It's connecting to the deepest truth of you and the life you are destined to live.

It's about you connecting to your TRUTH.

Your authenticity.

The unfolding of your expression.

Opening your heart up to more.

Desire comes from a place of surrender and the acceptance of who you are.

A little reflection here though, as sometimes your ego can get in the way of what you think you want and it may be the fantasy and the reality feel different. That's why connection to you is so important. Desires are heart energy but sometimes our ego, your head energy, takes over and what you think you might desire, may be driven by what you think you should be doing.

When you meet your desires and listen to your heart, it feels so right and there is an inner contentment with yourself. It's all about connection with yourself and the more you connect to your heart, to it's opening, the more you'll become familiar with the feeling of true connection and meet your desires - and if you don't, your body will tell you. Like with anything, the more you do it, the more it then becomes the norm and you will find yourself doing it without even thinking.

But what if you don't know?

Part of the reason you can struggle with desire is because you may feel unworthy of love and that you don't deserve what you desire. Part of this journey of exploration is to listen to your heart and identify what's there, to be honest with yourself about what happens when you think about something you desire. Is there fear? Is there something you are scared of that's stopping you believe it can be your reality.

When there's something your soul craves, the magnetic energy vibrating from your heart will start drawing it towards you, powerfully and quickly. The only way that thing (situation, person, opportunity, etc.) won't completely manifest for you is if you push it away by putting fear-based energy into the situation. This can be any resistant emotions such as anger, resentment, judgement, guilt, shame, whatever you do that places negative energy around it.

In opening your heart to discover what your heart desires, first you have to connect to the heart and open up the communication channels.

I trust my inner voice

It's important you LISTEN, but this can sometimes be tricky, especially if you keep yourself super busy and your mind feels overwhelmed. Making sacred space to listen to the longings, the callings, the singing of your heart and soul, will completely serve you. If you don't make the space, then the likelihood of you making your dreams a reality is slim.

Once you are able to listen to the signs, trusting them is the next step. The decisions are made on this inner connection, this inner knowing and this can feel super special. This doesn't come easy for most of us though. We lead busy lives and can spend too much time in our heads rather than in a place full of heart wisdom and knowing. You have to go within yourself to connect to your inner essence and, as with all the work you have been doing so far, all the parts of you've discovered and connected to. The more you listen, the deeper the connection you will have.

Do you dream?

I often have quite vivid dreams - ones that wake me up in the night. My dreams tend to come through as clear messages for me but often I don't remember anything at all after a good night's sleep. I do day dream though, and when I meditate, they can often take me off somewhere.

How often do you remember your dreams and are they something you believe in? If in the past, you have been told by someone your desires or dreams are unrealistic or unachievable, then may have started to dream small. When this happens, you limit yourself and put excuses in the way of you living your life in this heart space.

You can have it all when you believe it. The more we connect to the heart and the feeling of meeting it's desires and dreams, the more it will become your reality.

The first step in finding your heart's desire is to set the intention you will live your life this way. I know this may sound obvious, but few people ever make that decision. Know your original desires are still within you. Most people have buried them under a lot of resistance and beliefs that they may not be achievable. They then take you in the wrong direction. You want to get to a place where you communicate your desires often and be more specific, like: I will live by the sea one day.

This is a dream of mine and I absolutely know it will be my reality one day. I can feel it in my heart. It's what keeps it alive and I always speak to it with the knowing that it will happen. I even have a bank account called beach house and I save every month towards that dream. I know it's happening one day, it's a matter of when. I also have a dream that I will be on Loose Women one day (a TV show for women in the UK). I've actually seen myself on the show in my dreams and believe I will be on it one day. I talk about it a lot and say it's only a matter of time and I believe that. As I write this now, I have been contacted by Channel 4 to be on an upcoming documentary – it's not Loose Women, but it feels so aligned and I know I'm getting closer to my dream becoming a reality.

The journey of my expansion has led me to exploring all of my desires. I never knew that some of them were driven by fear but sometimes you have to do something, to know it's not want you want at all.

When I first tapped into my sexual energy, it was the same time I remembered trauma I had experienced in my past and I had no idea what to do with it. Rather than lean into it and embody it, I kept running and all the sexual energy I had suppressed for most of my adult life was coming back in bundles; it was overflowing and it was overwhelming.

It also happened around the same time as Helen passing away. I was in a place where I wanted to do everything now. I had all these feelings, these urges, these desires and I felt like there was no time to process. I felt like there wasn't any time. Time was running out and even though I didn't realise at the time, I was petrified I was going to die too, so it was now or never.

I met a friend one night for dinner, one of my beautiful friends I am always unapologetically me with. I explained how these urges were taking me over and how unsettled I felt. She then told me she had recently started exploring her sexuality and actually opening up her relationship and experiencing intimacy with other people. This totally excited me and although I felt quite unhinged with it, I wanted it NOW. I couldn't believe we were having this conversation, albeit with whispered voices in a restaurant, but it felt so refreshing to me.

I told her, I would love to experience something different too one day, and without even thinking, I suggested meeting up with them. I would speak to Mark and suggest the possibility of us trying swinging. It wasn't something I'd even considered before but I knew I needed something and this felt raw and exciting.

It's ok to speak my truth

OMG, could I really be saying this out loud? It felt so freeing, especially speaking to someone who actually understood.

So that's exactly what we did. We arranged it in a few days and it was the most liberating experience.

I had only ever kissed a woman once before, when I lived in Canada, and it was more to put a show on for the boys we were with. I remember thinking oooh, that was a bit different, and the boys loved it. I felt so ashamed the next day and put it down to a drunken crazy night out.

So here I was, not only kissing one of my friends. but also then all engaging with one another; kissing, caressing, whipping... we did lots, but we agreed to only have sex with our partners. It was like electricity and I was like wow, I have now found what I have been looking for. To explore, to expand outside of my relationship and to do all this in a safe environment, with people I knew, was perfect.

I felt sexy, I felt powerful and most importantly, I felt like me. And although it felt a bit frantic, I knew it was all part of my journey of exploring and that inner feeling felt grounding even though now I look back and know I wasn't grounded at all. I was totally living in my head. I was giving myself no space to lean into what I was feeling. I felt like I was on a rollercoaster all the time. I was running, I was definitely not breathing or having any time to contemplate and think about the impact it was having on me, let alone Mark.

Having Mark with me on this journey, kept me feeling safe and I was surprised how nice it was to see him let go and engage with another woman. I was surprised I never felt jealous and it felt special to share him. When we came back to the hotel, my goodness, how much did we want each other, we ripped each other clothes off and we made love. It was electric, my whole body pulsated with aliveness. We felt so much closer and appreciated each other so much more now we were all by ourselves.

But after this experience, I wanted more. I felt like I was a ticking time bomb and If I didn't do it now I never would have the chance. I joined an adult site, which was an eye opener and quickly realised this was a totally different level to where I was at, but with a big realisation there was a whole new world out there I was yet to explore.

I put together a profile. Mark helped and I told him I would love to explore time with other couples, it sounded like a lot of people did it and why not, we might learn something. So after lots of chatting to couples, some that were definitely not for us, we arranged to meet a couple for a drink with a view to seeing where it would take us.

Mark was like a rabbit in the headlights at the time. When I look back, I know I was ignoring him, I wasn't considering his feelings at all. I know he did all these meetings for me but I honestly didn't care. I never appreciated one of the reasons I felt free to do this was because he was by my side keeping me feeling safe so I could explore my sexuality. I thank my lucky stars every day I had met a man open to this new world. I dread to think how this would have played out and what would have happened if he said no. I know there was no stopping me. I also know he has learnt a lot from this time in our life and our relationship has gone to another level of intimacy. This was my truth then and it opened up a whole new world to me.

The next meet was again refreshing. We met another couple in a pub and talked quite openly about sex. I have always loved talking about sex, so to meet likeminded people was great. We got on well and agreed we would take it back to their hotel room. I honestly felt like I was on a movie set of some crazy porn film - what the hell was I doing?!

It was quite a fumble at the beginning as we all tried to interact with each other. I know now that I wasn't 100% in my body but I felt alive. I was being wild. I thought I didn't have long left, it was all so urgent and frantic!

This was the first time we swapped partners and actually slept with someone else in the same room as each other. I had a great connection with the guy I was with but I could see the awkwardness between Mark and the other woman. The connection wasn't here with them and at the end of the night, we took away the lesson that it wasn't about the physical act of sex, the energy had to be right. We both agreed after this meet, sleeping with someone else didn't add to the experience at all, again another lesson learnt.

We met with another couple after this and this was a very significant night. Early on that day, I had a session with my sex therapist and I remember her saying, why don't you consider waiting and giving yourself some space to see how you feel? I was addicted though and there was no stopping me.

We went through the motions again, drinks chatting and then we went into their hot tub, had lots of kissing and caressing and then went to their bedroom. I remember laying there in this big bubble of sexy interaction, I was being kissed all over my body whilst someone else was kissing my breasts and I had a HUGE light bulb moment and what I now know as an out of body experience. I saw myself on the bed and was looking down on myself and asked what the hell are you doing Kerry? You are not even enjoying this, this is happening to you and you are not even feeling it, what's the point? Why are you here? It was so loud, I remember getting up and saying I was ready to go.

I realised, what I was doing wasn't connecting to my desires at all. I was trying to numb myself again from feeling the sexual energy alive in me. I was disassociating myself from my body and I thought sex was the answer. It wasn't. I wasn't meeting myself with what I wanted. I was unhinged, ungrounded and wild and I wasn't being me. I was punishing myself and doing whatever I could to stop feeling it.

Mark and I talked at length about all the experiences and both decided swinging wasn't for us, it was boring and as I was the driver of everything, I knew deep down nothing was changing in me. I was an addict, going from one situation to the next to have my fix, but when I stopped and thought about it, I didn't feel empowered. I felt numb and I still wasn't feeling fulfilled.

As a couple, we learnt when there was a connection, we could explore with others and everything that we learnt, we always brought it back to us. It made us want each other more and appreciate what we did have. But most of the experiences we had were lacking in connection, they were an act of sex, disconnected from any emotion and although it took me to the edge off my wildness, it left me feeling totally unfulfilled. I was still searching for what would make me feel complete and it certainly wasn't here. What was I still looking for?

So at this point, I spent time asking myself what is it that I really desire? What do I want? It was clear I still felt this need to explore with others. I knew there was something quite special in me, exploring my sexuality, and I was getting braver to discuss other fantasies I had. Even though, I had learnt so much, I was still hungry for more. But now I wanted it on my terms, completely on my terms.

Whenever I fantasized about sexual encounters, I always had the same scenario in my head - having a threesome with two men. I felt it. I knew exactly how I wanted this to go and I knew I could make it happen. So I sat down with Mark and had a chat, but this time, I had started my tantric journey and was definitely starting to feel more in my power, communicating what I would like, what I didn't want and if something didn't feel right, then I would say. It was hard being honest with Mark. Often I would look at him and the look of "where has my girl gone" would be looking back at me. I think he was hoping this wild woman in me would be satisfied after all we had been through but it was just the beginning and now I was getting to the truth of what I wanted underneath all the crazy.

All those experiences happened in a space of about three months. It was a whirlwind, totally led by me and my urgency to explore and expand. I learnt so much but also realised this world was not for me. I enjoyed exploring my sexuality but I wasn't present and knew I wasn't getting what I wanted. I was now a few months into my Tantra massage training and was getting used to expressing how and where I wanted to be touched, how slow, how fast... It was all there to explored and my next experience was a whole new ball game to anything I had experienced before. I can honestly say it was one of the best sexual experiences of my life.

I arranged the threesome with the guy from a couple we had played with before. I knew I had a connection with him and Mark knew him too. It was in a hotel room. I had thought through everything. I wore a very sexy dress but also not that revealing. Underneath, I had a beautiful negligee that felt amazing, as well as some gorgeous knickers and bra. I felt so sexy. When we got into the room, I felt very nervous, again had one of the moments - can I really be doing this? - and was so glad Mark was with me. This wasn't for him but I felt so safe with him there.

I felt so powerful. I laid on the bed when I had enough of the small talk and said I wanted them to kiss me from the base of my feet all over with my clothes on. I was very clear on what wasn't ok, they were not to touch anything intimate. I wanted to be honoured exactly as I was, slowly, sensually and for them to listen to the instructions I was giving them. OMG, the power I felt was incredible!

I led the whole evening. I was in complete control of what I wanted, how the whole night went. I led the entire time, they listened and they served me. It was magical and an experience I will never ever forget. I came away feeling like I had been truly met and knowing I would absolutely repeat an experience like this again; it definitely wasn't Mark's thing but it was mine!

I am sharing these stories with you so you understand the journey I have been on to understand myself and the energy that was rising within me. Yes, I made so many mistakes along the way but I have learnt so much, about myself, about my sexuality and it's had a huge impact on my relationship. We have been through so much as a couple, from the point my past revealed itself to all the experiences we journeyed on together, to raw painful conversations about our truth. it's taken us in so many directions but hand on heart, I wouldn't change any of it for the world.

What I have realised too is it takes all sort of relationships to make the world go round and who says you must have one partner, that one person can meet you in everything you need, that you should always sleep in the same bed, with the same person your whole life. My relationship is still evolving, we have no label and no idea what is next for us. What I do know though, is when you surrender to the truth of who you are, you feel comfortable to share your voice with others and live a life that feels whole and connected and that wins every time over being numb.

Can you see now, why sexual energy for me has been such a huge part of my awakening and me getting to know myself? From the moment it arrived, I tried to squash it down and release it through sex. It connected me to my body, it gave me the power to explore my sexuality and explore my desires. It helped set me free from the trauma my body had experienced.

It's the fundamental piece, the powerful life energy that connects it all together and although I've introduced you to its power, this is just the beginning. I am not suggesting you go off and have wild explorations in sex, that was my truth and this is about connecting to yours.

Are you ready to explore and expand into your heart now and see what it desires?

Connection Exercises:

1) Heart Breathing

As the heart is another powerful energy centre of the body, doing focussed breathing around the heart can deepen your connection. This type of breath work is perfect when you are overwhelmed or know you are very much in your head. It can also help you to open your heart up to receive, connect more deeply to emotion, to love and to what you really feel.

- With this type of breathing, bring all your focus to the heart and breathe a little deeper than normal.
- As you take a breath, inhale and breathe in to the centre of your heart, and as you exhale let the breath expand in your heart centre.
- As you exhale, feel into what the expansion represents. Is it letting go of anything in the way of you feeling or is it expanding the heart centre so you can receive more deeply into your heart? They are both similar and represent expansion and the opening of your heart. It's about what the focus is for you.
- If it feels a bit odd and you don't feel like the focus is there, place your hand over your heart and breathe into that as it may help you bring focus to it.

The world is holding you

2) Uncover your heart's desires

This is a journaling exercise for you to connect to your desires. Pick a question you are drawn to and let yourself run wild with your expression. If there is a question that makes you want to run away, that's probably the one you should pick. Be patient and if you feel like nothing is flowing, try doing it a different day.

If you feel like there is big resistance to doing this exercise, use the EAM and ask do I have resistance to doing this exercise? Then follow the 5 steps and release the resistance.

Give yourself a time frame. Keep the pen moving and allow any and all responses to come, even if they don't make sense. Write until you feel like you've expressed yourself.

- What is my heart's deepest desire?
- What would I love to do that I've never admitted to anyone?
- What's missing or lacking in my life?
- What would make my heart sing?
- What do I secretly long to be, do or have?
- Wouldn't it be nice/fabulous/amazing if_________?
- If I let myself dream, I would _______________.
- What gets in the way of me dreaming?

Now try the heart breathing again but this time, ask your heart energy some questions:

- Get yourself comfortable and place your hand on your heart or bring your focus to it.

- Take a few deep breaths in and out of the heart centre and ask - What do I want?
- Spend some time listening and acknowledge what pops into your mind and then ask - What do I **really** want? Express this in a sentence, a word, see what arises. This is about you and nobody else.
- Then spend some time considering what can you do to support your desire and meet it in YOU
- If this feels too much, start with gratitude and ask - What am I grateful for right now?
- When you shift from desire to gratitude, you are already creating what you want by appreciating what you already have.

AWAKEN & LOVE YOUR BODY

Learning how to get into my body has had such an impact on my entire world. That's what the word embodiment is all about, embodying everything that is alive in you. I had no idea this was a thing when I started this journey of awakening. I had spent years not feeling very good about my body and the thought of actually loving it was never an option because all I ever wanted was a different one.

In this chapter, we are going to be looking at the relationship you have with your body and how you can learn to love it more deeply and feel more. I never thought of my body as a sacred part of me that I should show love to; all I ever did was put it down and try to change it in some way.

Learning to love your body is another piece of accepting yourself exactly as you are and the more you do, the more it will become a way of life. Don't waste time and emotions staring at pictures of perfect bodies and wishing to be one of them. If you need visual inspiration, find photos of you at your best, not someone else at their best.

Beauty is the light that shines from within

Recognise and accept that you may not look the same as you did before you had kids but maybe you get to a place where you accept yourself as you are now, a place where you look at your body with love and don't spend your time saying awful things about it. Love energy is high vibration and enables the energy to flow; the more love you give it, the more you notice.

Always love yourself first and the rest will follow. Beauty is the light that shines from within and the more you connect with the light, the more you can find peace within yourself. It's a journey though and one that takes time. And the first step is understanding how you feel in the first place.

How do you feel about your body? This isn't the time to hide from your truth, be honest with yourself.

Do you love and accept ALL of you?

I never loved my body. I think back to my teenage years and I was disgusted by it and spent my life comparing myself to others wishing I had smaller thighs, smaller boobs, less spots, anything else but what I had.

When I was bullied, I thought it was because I was fat and looked so horrific to everyone else. It was the story I told myself. I was constantly on a diet, had bulimia for years, tried everything and even when I lost so much weight, I felt no different. My clothes were baggy but I was still fat in my mind. It didn't matter what anyone told me, I didn't believe them.

I'll tell you a funny story, well it's funny to me now anyway. A group of boys called me donkey when I was growing up. I have no idea how it started but every time I saw them, they would shout out 'alright donkey, eeyore eeyore'. I hated it and thought it was because I was fat. This happened throughout my teens and then when I went to university, my friends threw me a leaving party. It was a big deal for me to be going to university and it was so nice to have a such a big send off. That night, I was all dolled up and actually plucked up the courage to ask one of them why they are called me it and they told me it was because I was tall, like the arsenal footballer Tony Adams that had the same nickname. I was so shocked. How stupid had I been?! I had spent all these years in turmoil as I thought they called me a donkey because I was fat - even though I wasn't fat at all, it was all in my mind and I had told myself that story for years. It continued into my adulthood, but this time, I wasn't consciously telling myself these things. I used to go to the gym all the time and not out of enjoyment most of the time. It was the only way I felt ok, otherwise I felt disgusting. I invested in so many lotions and potions to make myself feel better about my body. I had drawers full but I'd never use them as I thought it would be wasted on me, that I wasn't good enough to actually use them and spoil myself in this way, so they stayed there, collecting dust.

I told those stories to myself for so many years and without even knowing it, they were affecting the way I felt about my body. I remember, from a young age, using a role of tape and wrapping it round my thighs to try and make them slimmer. I was disgusted with my body, especially my thighs – thunder thighs I called them. I was so horrid to myself all of the time.

This carried on right into my twenties, but no one knew what I really felt as it was this secret internal battle I had. I thought it was 'normal' to feel like this. The turning point came for me when I worked with a life coach. We were sitting in a beautiful hotel in London. I had never had a coach before so wasn't used to being asked questions about myself. Silke was a friend and colleague from work and I was only doing it at first to help her out, but I remember this conversation so well. We were talking about my need to be so busy and that I was so tired. I was working so hard and going to the gym all the time. It was the only thing that made me feel good and if I didn't go to the gym, I felt so terrible. She asked me how I would feel if the gym closed for a week. I said I wouldn't be able to cope, the thought actually made me feel sick, but why?

If I didn't go to the gym, I felt so fat and disgusting. It made my body bearable to me. If I didn't go, I was lazy and no wonder I looked like I did. It gave me food for thought. I definitely became more aware of myself and started listening to my thoughts and understanding the stories I was telling myself. No wonder I felt so rubbish whenever I considered my body, saw myself in pictures or even caught a glimpse of myself in the mirror.

But nothing changed after that. I knew it felt so awkward but it's only now, six years later that I realise it was another pivotal moment I chose to ignore, and off I popped, back on to the hamster wheel until it arose again a couple of years later.

What it all came down to though is this - I struggled to receive love, especially from myself. It was something I constantly deflected from myself, almost like it was a bad thing to think nice things about yourself. I remember at school, people always saying 'Oh look at her, she totally loves herself' to someone that seems confident with their body. Now I would give that person a high five and say good for you, although the truth is many people that look like they love themselves don't at all, deep down.

So how do you nourish your body?

Another element of loving yourself that I never gave much thought to is how do I fuel my body. My entire life, I had always been on diets and was bulimic throughout my teenage years. I also suffered from IBS. I know the reason for that was definitely down to the trauma I had suppressed but I also had a dislike to food as I thought it made me fat or left me running for the loo at the most inconvenient times. Food became this huge inconvenience to me as it was something I never stopped thinking about and was never in a way that served me.

I heard something once and it stayed with me. Fuel your body like you would a car; you wouldn't put water in a car and expect it to work well, so don't neglect your own nourishment. It makes total sense and I have noticed a direct link with the food and drink I consume and the way I not only feel about my body, but also how I feel in myself. This is something I have become more and more aware of since I discovered the world of energy. If you put rubbish in, you get rubbish out and it is so true.

How do you fuel your body? Do you treat yourself to nutritious food which makes you feel good or do you know that you absolutely don't look after yourself in this way?

I love my food and it's a huge part of my life but in a positive way now. Having the awareness of what feels good and what doesn't has made a big difference to me. During lockdown, we did a vegan cookery course with my friend Nicola, from The Kleen Kitchen, and although I'm not completely converted yet, I have never learnt so much about food and the difference in my energy is amazing. It isn't an inconvenience anymore; it's a way of life and another way to give love to myself - and I am all about more ways to give love. Can you see how self-love can come in so many different ways?

Understanding your cycles

I always hated my periods. They were such an inconvenience to me and they were fuelled with so much shame. I started my period on holiday and I was gutted. My aunty Vi had taken me and my sister to Euro Disney. It was the first week it opened and we were so excited. We go to our hotel and it had a lovely pool. We checked in, I went to the loo and discovered my first ever period had arrived. I remember feeling disgusted and was so embarrassed to tell my aunt. She had to go to reception and get me some sanitary towels. I was so upset; no swimming pool for me. I went to a girl's secondary school for the most part of my education and I remember trying to hide my sanitary products so no one knew I was on. Always hiding parts of myself. A few years ago, a friend recommended I read *Period Power, by Maisie Hill.* Such a powerful book and It transformed the way I felt about my periods and in my late thirties, I started to feel so grateful and amazed by what my body was capable of each month. The biggest take outs I took from the book was understanding the different stages of my cycle and how I felt in each one. Here is a little summary of what happens in mine:

Winter – This is the start of my bleed and when I am here, I am in a restful nourishing space and want to wrap myself up in a cocoon and shut the world out. I look within lots and ask myself, what do I need right now and what's coming up in me? In my winter, I avoid speaking gigs and anything too visible.

Spring – as I come out of my bleed, it feels like spring, like I am waking up from a fog. Things become easier and I feel more energetic and motivated to do things. What do I want to do in my life and what do I want to learn? Something to watch out for here is that I feel so awake I find it hard to concentrate and get easily distracted by others and the wonderful things I could be doing in the world.

Summer – This is when I am on fire, I am so bloody excited by life. I am firing on all cylinders and I think I can achieve anything. Everything feels in flow and I love to be visible. If I was going to do a post that was a bit controversial, it would be now as I am happy to be seen by the world. What I need to be careful of here is over committing myself and saying yes to everything - in my summer, everything seems possible, but Autumn is nearly here.

Autumn – I start to feel less productive here as I prepare for my hibernation (in Winter). I am definitely more deep in thought and can be quite sensitive too. If I carry on with the hyper activity of summer, I definitely start to feel it here. Beware of my wrath too, when I'm in this place. I can quite easily lose my rag and my self-critic comes out to play too.

I have got to know my cycle so well now, I plan my life around it and it has made such a huge difference. Around the same time, I also found using tampons uncomfortable - as if my body was rejecting tampons - and I didn't feel comfortable using towels so I started using a moon cup. If you don't know what I mean, look it up. It's a small cup that collects the blood and you can reuse each time. It's so much better for the environment and although it took some getting used too, feels super comfortable now.

Does any of this resonate with you and your cycles? What are yours like?

Have you moved your body today?

Get your butt moving

The more you get your butt moving, the more you will awaken every single cell of your beautiful being. Ever since, I trained in Tantra Massage, movement has been a daily part of my life. I've always been active but this is different, it's about the intention that goes with it.

By intention, I mean spending a moment before you begin and asking yourself:

- What do I want to get out of this practice?
- Is it to wake my body up?
- Is it to stop me feeling yukky?
- Is it to move some stuck energy?
- Is it to feel the magic of embodiment?

In The Goddess Awakening® programme, I lead embodiment sessions every week and we connect to rage, blissful pleasure, to pain, joy, sexual energy and everything is welcomed. The practices give the goddesses the time to acknowledge what the body is saying and to give permission to feel it, to work with the energy that's moving through them. They are so powerful.

We do all sorts of movement to facilitate this release and awakening in you. The trick is to not take it too seriously. To do things that surprise your body, jump, shake, crawl, get all animalistic. I know you might be reading this thinking what?! Try it.

Think about the innocence children have. They don't care what they look like, so why should you? Remember the saying, dance like no one's watching? Get yourself moving. It's so powerful and something I recommend you do every day. It takes no time at all to moving your butt with some focussed intention and throwing some breath and sound in the mix too, it can transform your energy in minutes.

So let's start to explore your body with the following exercises:

Connection Exercises:

1) What's your body confidence story?

This is a journaling exercise for you to explore your relationship with confidence and your body. Even if you are in a place where you feel body confident, you may still hold on to resistance from your past that is stopping you from loving yourself even more. I invite you to do this exercise and explore what's there.

- A nice way to start this would be to think about a timeline of your life (including now) and make a note of times when you've had some negative self-talk about yourself, it could be when you had a baby or when you were friends with someone you thought was 'perfect' so you used to put yourself down.
- Spend some time exploring all of these moments in your life and make note of any negative thoughts or patterns you've seen emerging throughout your life.
- Look at the positive times of your story and make note of those too. How did you feel then? Can you remember any details of what you may have been doing then for you to feel this way?
- Using EAM, go through all the negative and positive

parts of your timeline, do I have any resistance to clear from this time in my life? Also notice if anything happens to the energy in your body and go through the 5 steps to clear it.

2) Dance your socks off

Don't underestimate the power of movement to get into your body. You can do this in so many ways - pick a song you LOVE and go for it. Don't hold back, give yourself permission to dance your socks off. It's a great idea to get yourself a nice playlist together and I am sharing some of my favourite ones with you on the bonus page (www.kerryosullivan.co.uk/book).

When you feel like you've had enough, spend some time in stillness, close your eyes and feel the energy in your body. How does it feel? Breathe it in and know if emotions arise, let them.

Movement is a fabulous way to release anything you are holding on to - you can always carry on for another song or carry on in stillness and enjoy how it feels in your body.

3) Listen and connect with each part of your body

Spend some time with yourself and connect to each part of your body. There is so much depth to this and so much you can learn from slowing things right down:

- Start by taking a few breaths and then start slowly scanning your body – start at the base of your feet and work your way up the body, not missing anything.
- What did you notice?

- Did anything feel tense or did you notice any sensations arising?
- Continue to breathe the whole time, noticing if anything shifts and changes as you do so.
- Do this as few times before you drop into stillness and notice how it feels to take this time with yourself.

SURRENDER TO PLEASURE

Oooh pleasure, this is one of my favourite topics but I used to think pleasure was a dirty word and not something you should actually enjoy. I had no idea. Are you open to pleasure now? Or does it feel out of reach for you? Pleasure is all there to be received when you are ready. In this chapter, I'm going to show you some steps you can take to surrender to all the pleasure and receive more of it in your life.

Now you've started to connect more deeply to your body and beginning to love and accept who you are, you may already have noticed you are experiencing more embodiment and more feelings may be arising in you. If this still feels really icky and you've been dreading this element and have some beliefs pleasure is not for you, please know my darling, it absolutely is. It is your birth right to experience all the pleasures and there is no end to how much you can experience. There is soooo much.

Your pleasure, your turn on

So what does pleasure look like for you and is it something you experience? Pleasure comes in so many forms; it can be from treating yourself to some ice cream and savouring every bit as you lick yourself around the cone, dancing and feeling how it feels in your body, or being present with your children and noticing how it feels when you see them laugh and smile and giving yourself permission to feel all the feels.

In this chapter, I am going to focus on self-pleasure as I believe it always starts with you. The more pleasure you receive in your body, the more you will be open to receive in life. It will transform how you feel about yourself, your relationships, your business, EVERYTHING. There is no end to the depths you can go to, depending on how much you give yourself permission to feel, to experience and to embody this delicious energy.

Self-pleasure was never part of my life until three years ago. I thought it was disgusting to touch yourself. Why would you do that? I thought it was wrong. I felt that disgusted with the thought of self-pleasure and I never did it for the first 37 years of my life.

I think I had this disconnect with my body as I associated that area with the trauma I'd gone through growing up. I didn't love my body and didn’t love who I was. I was ashamed of myself for never speaking, honouring myself, for never talking about what I felt. I was embarrassed I didn't know how to show love to myself and didn’t know how to receive love from anyone else either.

So, when I started my Tantra Journey and trained in Tantra Massage, I learnt how to connect to my body. I learnt how to be witnessed and seen in all of my expression and I learnt to appreciate it exactly as it was.

I released the shame I felt, I forgave myself for all the years I ignored myself,- especially my yoni. I ignored the pain and her yearning to be witnessed. It was just too painful for me.

When I realised self-pleasuring was something I had missed out on for most of my life. I carried so much shame around it, I knew I had some catching up to do. I signed up to OMG YES, which was a course based in US that taught you how to pleasure yourself. It was amazing and there were live videos of lots of inspirational women showing us how they touched themselves and how they turned themselves on. It was so liberating and was amazing for me as it made me realise it was ok to do it and all I needed to do was practice.

A few months later, I found a course in London - a weekend which was all about self-pleasure and orgasmic empowerment. It opened me up to a whole new realm and was another new experience for me. Although I had received a lot of pleasure from others, through food, through music, through spending time with those I love, but never from myself, well not to be a point of fulfilment anyway and I always knew it as an area I was due to explore.

I remember the first time I touched myself and realised it felt nice. I remember it so well. I was in the bath, no idea what age I was, I felt so naughty and almost ashamed I was doing it. I told myself it was wrong to touch myself and I never did it again. I remember speaking with a friend and she mentioned she couldn't wait to get home to self-pleasure. I told her I didn't do it and she nearly fell off her chair. "What do you mean?"

she said, "You don't touch yourself?". I then felt ashamed that I didn't.

In my twenties, I got myself a rabbit (one of the famous vibrators at the time) at an Ann Summers party. I remember when it arrived thinking what the hell do I do with that? I was mortified. I used it with my partner and never on my own.

When my marriage broke up, I tried again but my mind wouldn't shut up...now it was 'ah what a shame you have to do it on your own. Why are you so desperate for an orgasm? Should you be doing this Kerry?'. I stopped trying. Then when I discovered the world of Tantra, I realised it was an area I was still avoiding and if I now loved myself, why wasn't this part of my life. Whenever I tried to self-pleasure, there had to be some other kind of other stimulus; using toys, watching porn or being watched. There is nothing wrong with using stimulus but as I was becoming more aware of energy, I knew I was in my head. I was trying to get to a goal, to release the frustration I felt and meet the yearning I felt deep inside my yoni and even after I orgasmed, I was still left feeling unfulfilled.

When I saw the course, I knew it was for me; this was what I had been looking for, to be empowered by my own orgasmic vitality. We all have the tools to do this and it seems absolutely crazy to me this is not something that was ever encouraged. Well it is for some of us, I'm sure, but I also know we are a nation of self-critics and to touch ourselves, to love our bodies can sometimes bring up shame, guilt, embarrassment and even disgust. I have felt all those things but during that weekend, I felt so beautiful. My body felt so amazing. I felt sexy, I felt vibrant and I felt alive.

During the workshop, I felt my G spot and my cervix for the first time and I remember being blown away as it was a lot bigger then I imagined when aroused. I felt the beauty of it, in all its forms; the beautiful ridges, felt its energy, felt it pulsate and felt the life force within it. My yoni enjoyed it and the peacefulness inside, like the sunshine had popped from behind the clouds.

I felt the waves of relaxation as my body softened. I felt my yoni expand, felt its opening. It thanked me for taking my time, for being gentle and acknowledging how it wanted to be touched. I will never forget it, the moment when I met myself like this for the first time.

I felt alive, but this feels so different, slower and softer like a rose bud beginning to open. Over the weekend, we did a number of guided practices where I touched myself in a room full of other amazing souls doing the same. The space was held so beautifully, I felt myself surrender and I felt so proud of myself.

I connected to my breath, I moved and rocked my pelvis, I let myself say what I wanted to say. I never held back. It wasn't about reaching orgasm, it was about experiencing pleasure. I loved how it made me feel. I felt so liberated and my whole body was pulsating with tingles. I wrote this after we had finished and then later I read it to the room of people I had journeyed with:

"Wow. I did that all by myself. I found my own pleasure with my fingers and I have felt fulfilment within me.

To enjoy touch, to really listen, to expand my throat and voice and say what I wanted to say. I pleasured myself and was not in my head but in my body.

My body is beautiful.

My energy is mine.

I have all I need within me.

I am a butterfly and I am free.

Free from myself and any of the expectations I have always put on myself.

I'm flying higher and find myself on another level once again.

Kerry you are truly amazing; I love you."

It was such a beautiful and liberating experience. We spend so much time rushing around, what if we made self-pleasure one of our priorities like eating, drinking and brushing our teeth. It's been a part of my life for a few years now and I want you to know it wasn't something that came easy to me.

I have been on a journey with pleasure and I still am. I would love a world where everyone is empowered to love who they are, every part of them. What a wonderful world it would be, based on the foundation of self-love and orgasmic vitality.

It's not about where you're going, it's about experiencing the now

Over the last few years, pleasure and exploring the depths of my sexuality has been my focus in everything. I've attended sexuality festivals and just before lockdown, I attended the most amazing tantric shamanic retreat called Master Your Pleasure, in Goa, India.

This was next level for me and I had some huge shifts there; one in particular I'm still integrating over a year later. Over the week, we explored and embodied pleasure, mostly alone, and I had what I can only describe as an out of body experience, connecting to consciousness. It was phenomenal and pleasure on a different scale. I lifted out of my body and surrendered to the light. Giving myself permission to embody pleasure has opened me up for deeper experiences and has enhanced my connection to spirit too.

- So how does the word Pleasure feel for you?
- I would love to you to close your eyes and say PLEASURE out loud.
- How does your body react when you say it?
- Now say it a little slower and notice how it feels?

It may surprise you but sometimes, even the word can make people feel awkward, so if you do, don't worry about it; acknowledging all the feels is why you are here.

In the last chapter, when you began the exploration of your body and completed the body honouring exercise, how did this feel? Did you take much time to acknowledge how your body felt? Take a moment now – did it feel yummy or did it feel uncomfortable? Breathe into whatever arises.

Honouring yourself in this way and having an understanding how something feels is a form of self-pleasure. The depths you can go to and experience are down to your ability to receive this love from yourself, so it's good to have this awareness first before we explore this some more.

Receiving pleasure is an act of self-love and if you've only scratched the surface with how you receive this. I invite you to deepen this practice with yourself, to tap into the juicy energy and see whether this makes a difference to the experience when you set the intention to receive.

One of the things that helped me explore this further was knowing that in order to give love fully to others, I had to open my heart more to receive love from myself. I knew there was always more room to deepen this love.

So, how do you like to be touched?

To receive and allow pleasure, understanding of how you like to be touched is a great thing to explore. If you don't know how you like to be touched, how can you possibly show someone else how?

Are you are yearning for soft and gentle touch to make you feel nourished and tingle with excitement? Would you like firmer touch like your head massaged or to pull on your hair to release tension and awaken you? Our bodies give us signals. If you give yourself some time each day to be with your body, you will begin to notice more.

In the world of Tantra and sacred sexuality, connection to pleasure isn't about reaching an end goal, it's all about being completely present with what's happening in that moment.

Breathe through your pussy

It's about Connection. It's about receiving and embodying the experience and not about where you are going.

If you are used to using stimulus in a self-pleasure practice, like porn or imagery, you are more likely to be leading from your head energy and may have goal in place to achieve an orgasm. Although there is nothing wrong with this, when you remove the goal and stimulus that can distract you, you become more connected to your body and what it's experiencing. The head, heart and hara energy centres are expanded as you embody more of what you are feeling.

Always remember the principles of breath, sound and movement as this will enable the energy to move around the body, so it's not concentrated in one particular area, and you will start to feel pleasure in other areas too, which can feel delicious. It will also enable the body to release any resistance it is holding so it you can completely surrender to receiving touch.

Let's talk about orgasms

Orgasms are not just about pleasure. It is an important aspect of women's health and wellbeing as it releases the love hormone oxytocin which helps you feel relaxed, lifts your mood and connects you to the divine. It's when you are most in flow and when you are in the state of orgasm, nothing else matters. Orgasms are the sweet spot of pure divinity for me and every woman's right is to receive all the orgasms. I have one most days and it's delicious.

There are lots of types of orgasms but let me introduce you to a few: Clitoral, G spot and a full body orgasm.

Clitoral Orgasms - The clitoral orgasm is the most commonly spoken about and a lot of women say they need clitoral stimulation in order to reach orgasmic states. The Clitoris has over 8000 nerve endings, more than the head of a man's lingam (penis), and can be beautifully stimulated in lots of ways; through light or firm touch, through friction and rubbing or through stimulus with a toy or even in the shower as the water touches it. It's extremely sensitive and its purpose, my lovelies, if you chose to accept it, is to provide you with the upmost pleasure!

One of my biggest ahas when exploring my clitoris was she was way bigger than the sensitive 'doorbell' at the top of the vulva. The clitoris has legs that extend down deep into the vagina and can be stimulated through the labia, which opened up a whole new world for me. Sometimes the glands under the hood of the clitoris can be extremely sensitive and sometimes painful if over stimulated or dry, so to explore the fullness of it, use a water based lubricant or an oil, like coconut or jojoba, to explore when you are enjoying a self-pleasure practice. Take your time too and explore all of her because areas that may seem numb, may come alive when you start to explore her more.

G Spot Orgasms - The G spot, also referred to as the urethral sponge and female prostate and, in the Tantra world, often referred to as the 'goddess' spot, which I love! The G spot is located on the front wall away from the vagina entrance and under the arch of the pubic bone.

Contrary to the name, it is not a 'spot'. It is two to three inches of erectile tissue and has a rough rigid texture when aroused. It's easier to locate in certain positions and if you can start by placing one or two fingers inside your vagina with the pads up and curl your fingers in a 'come here' type gesture, you may be able to find it. Remember though, as it's erectile tissue, it will grow and expand when you are aroused and without arousal, you may not feel it. Another thing to bear in mind is, as it surrounds the urethra, stimulating it may make you feel like you need to run to the loo. That type of sensation may get some getting used to and may not be something you even enjoy. Relax and experiment with the different sensations and surrender into everything you feel.

Energy Orgasms/Full Body Orgasms – these are one of my favourite types of orgasm to share and experience as they are so deliciously embodied. You can have the most amazing full body orgasms without even touching yourself at all - just using your breath, giving yourself permission to make sounds and moving your body.

This type of orgasm takes patience though as it may take some time to get out of your head and drop into your body. Using all the elements of breath, sound and movement are so vital in allowing the energy to move through your body. I find it easier when I play music that stimulates the senses and adds to the sensations. If you fancy giving this a go, I'd set a timer for yourself as it will help you focus. Start with your breath, being aware of your body and setting the intention of full body pleasure, try not to overthink it. Lie down or stand up, close your eyes and start and see what it brings. The biggest challenge that crops up for me is switching my head off but the more you practice, the more you will drop in.

Pleasure Toys

There are many views in the world of sacred sexuality on using pleasure toys. I love them and am so grateful for every sensation

I have felt using them. They have opened my eyes to so much more pleasure, especially at the beginning when I was so scared to use my own fingers. It felt like such a huge step for me.

If the thought of pleasure toys scares you, it's ok as there are so many to choose from and they may be something that's not for you either. It's one of the topics no one ever taught me and what works for someone, may do nothing to someone else, so I would always recommend trying some. It's a great way to understand what you like and whether they are for you or not.

***Yoni Eggs* -** One of the ways I learnt how to receive pleasure and connect to my pussy was to use a yoni egg. The yoni egg is a polished stone in the shape of an egg, created to be inserted into your vagina. They are made of a stone / crystals which emit their own vibrational healing energy or frequency. Therefore, you choose your yoni egg depending on your intention. Black obsidian yoni eggs are incredibly powerful with transformational energy. This egg is said to strengthen the root chakra, the seat of all of our issues with feeling safe and knowing you are enough. Obsidian is a grounding stone and connects us to our power and the energy of Mother Earth. Rose quartz, which is my favourite, is all about love; love for your body, love for your partner, and love for your spirit and life. Rose quartz emits a beautiful healing energy of calm and may help you feel more connected to your divine self than ever before.

Having a yoni egg practice is an alternative to common Kegel exercises, you may strengthen your vaginal muscles and benefits include: decreased incontinence, retoning post-childbirth, increased orgasms and of course, connection to your pussy and the power house she is.

Are you ready to explore your expansion into pleasure?

Do not use a Yoni Egg if you are pregnant or wearing an IUD though. Yoni eggs come in different sizes, small, medium and large. You may wish to purchase a box set of all 3. The size you choose to work with will change as you go deeper in your practice. You may choose to start with a larger egg and then work your way down to a smaller egg as your muscles tighten. When you start a yoni egg practice, make it a ritual and part of your self-pleasure and choose whether you want to add any extra stimulus to the practice or not. When I first got mine, I had no idea and used to pop it in whilst working and think I was doing my yoni egg practice. It's all about intention so set one before you begin.

I love my small bullet vibrators. They are effective and are great, both playing on my own and with a partner. My glass dildo feels so sacred and what's so delicious about glass is you can warm it up or cool it down in the freezer, and it adds another dimension entirely to a pleasure session. I also have a toy I use as my quick fix and during the days of the lockdown, it was my saviour. It's called the Wand and I am not even joking when I say I can orgasm in less than 5 minutes with the wand BUT (and this is a big but) the orgasms for me feel quite superficial and they are nowhere near as fulfilling as a full session of embodied pleasure.

There are so many great toys out there, including some fabulous one to explore the anus too. Do your own research - I've recommended a few sites on the bonus page that you can begin your exploration (www.kerryosullivan.co.uk/book) and see what toys speak to you. Get one ordered and see what happens. I would recommend these are not used all the time though as they can be distracting and there is also so much pleasure to be explored without them. Some women report they've desensitised their body, although it's not something I have ever experienced. They are most definitely worth exploring though.

Do you find it hard to orgasm?

This is a common problem with a lot of women and my view is, it all comes down to connection to self and how present you can allow yourself to be in the moment. I also want to throw in here that orgasms are not the only pleasure to be experienced. If you find it hard to orgasm, you may also find it hard to receive pleasure. You can still have a juicy exploration and beautifully nourishing play with yourself without any orgasms at all. It's about dropping the goal of orgasm and setting the intention of pleasure in all its forms and getting yourself in the mood to explore:

- Give yourself space and time to drop into the moment.
- Connect to your breath and if you find yourself distracted by thoughts and feel quite heady, breathe more and try some pussy and heart breaths to help activate the sexual energy so it moves through you.
- Remove all the goals.
- Keep an open mind and give yourself permission to feel.

Kink took my pleasure to a whole new level

I first experienced kink on my first sexuality gathering at Osho Leela. It was the most mind blowing week of workshops that expanded my mind and body. The biggest eye opener was learning all about the world of kink and actually discovering I quite enjoyed whipping someone and receiving it too. It was so much fun and it's not something I have ever experimented with, especially with someone I didn't know. I felt powerful, I felt beautiful and in complete devotion of the person I was serving. Little did I know, this workshop would trigger me. The laughter and fun from the workshop quickly faded when I headed for lunch. I felt like I wanted to cry and didn't know why.

Over the course of the day, even though I had worked on my sexual assault when I was 17, I had never worked on the physical pain I experienced back then. Here I was, enjoying pleasure through pain and it didn't feel right - that wasn't pain, not like I experienced back then. Later that day, I attended the most profound workshop with an amazing teacher, Elaine Yonge. We worked with a partner and witnessed each other's Yonis. It sounds crazy but my goodness, it was so powerful. We tapped into this energy and thought of what we would like to say. I wanted to say sorry for never connecting to that part of my body and for not honouring myself enough all those years ago to acknowledge what had happened and to never tell a soul. I cried, I screamed and released the trauma from my body and released all the pain I'd kept in for the last 21 years.

I felt like I was in a trance, the trauma released with shaking, but I wasn't resisting it anymore and instead I was picturing my freedom - me as the beautiful butterfly - as this all left my body. The space was beautifully held for me; my face was held, I was told I was safe, I was loved and I was going to be free. Wow, what an experience. And another reminder of why I am doing the work I do now. I want everyone to be free of past trauma because when you release it, the feeling of freedom is phenomenal. When I got up on the stage on my last night and sang *I Believe I Can Fly*, it meant the world to me. What an unexpected journey I had been on in five days in this perfect location, in the Dorset countryside.

After that experience of kink, even though it triggered me, I was so intrigued to explore the relationship between pain and pleasure, so I signed up to a day of sensual conscious kink. This time, the setting was in a beautiful yurt, in a field near Brighton. It was an intimate group and in some ways it felt safe but it also meant there was no hiding. So, what's sensual conscious kink? I didn't know what it meant. I knew about BDSM (bondage, discipline, dominance, submission, and sadomasochism - think *Fifty Shades,* if you don't know what it means). A combination of sensual and kink sounded like the perfect match for me and wow, what a day I had, full of so much desire and fulfilment. I felt so blessed to have experienced it.

One of the questions I was asked during the workshop was how did I want to be touched? I am normally ok with this question in one of my Tantra workshops but in this setting, there was so much to explore, so much depth and so many ideas. I had experienced quite a few toys and types of kinky touch in the bedroom with Mark but never in this intimate setting where I had so much choice to explore the depths and edges of myself.

Over lunch, I was feeling a little impatient and eagerly waiting for more experience but I was also in deep reflection about my life at home and how much I loved Mark and the journey we are on together. It's so much softer and we are so considerate of each other now.

I always get asked, how does he let you do this stuff on your own? Is he ok with it?

The real truth is, he is. And we talk about everything from both of our perspectives. I remember when I had that crazy period where I definitely didn't considered Mark as much as I do now, it was all about me and the craziness I was feeling inside. It's now more about us both. We consider each other and we listen, we communicate and we hear each other.

So, back to the yurt. I was most definitely outside of my comfort zone but I was intrigued, excited and felt very connected to myself. I decided I would be happiest going last so I could learn from others and feel into it a bit more.

The thing is, I have had so many ideas in my head about scenes I would love to play out, fantasies and dreams, but the thought of it being a reality is something else.

Being in a giving role was always a default for me and I loved being able to explore a more dominant side of myself. I have always been quite dominant in character but also quite enjoy being in more submissive role. I think it all depends on what mood I am in and that's the joy of knowing yourself and how you are feeling from moment to moment.

Now it was my turn. I felt like I had waited forever for this moment. I knew exactly what I wanted but I was scared to communicate it at first, I suppose it was fear of judgement, fear of them thinking 'blimey, she wants that?!'

I had a word with myself though as I was so nervous but knew this was the ideal space for me to try this. It was ok if I didn't like it and could stop it at any time. I was in complete control here and once I had communicated it, I felt so empowered. I had visualised this picture of myself and here I was asking for it.

I had the most beautiful rose gold collar on with gold studs on, I was spanked, my hair was pulled and the most erotic words were whispered in my ears. The beautiful beings I worked with were amazing. They were so present. They met me and did exactly what I wanted, said the words I wanted to hear. The space was wonderfully held and I explored all the edges of this experience.

I experienced pain, so much pleasure and I was awakened through all of myself. It was exhilarating, pulsating every part of me. I was alive. I was met with everything I desired and I felt euphoric.

Wow, wow, wow, how did it all happen in 15 minutes?

Afterwards, I asked for some space, I didn't want to be touched. I wanted to feel the ripples of the pleasure through me. After a few minutes, I asked to be held and feel the warmth of the people that had given me everything I desired. As soon as I left, I felt my body yearning for home and for Mark and had this urge for me to experience it all again with him.

On my way home, I listened to the radio – the first two songs were perfect for the way I was feeling, first the pointer sisters – I'm so excited.... I felt every word and sang my heart out ' *I'm so excited, and I just can't hide it. I'm about to lose control and I think I like it'* followed by Lisa Stansfield's Change, which made me cry with happiness – *'If I could change the way, I live my life today, I wouldn't change a single thing'*.

Absolutely perfect songs for how I was feeling in the moment and knew I wouldn't change a thing. My first experience of conscious sensual kink certainly opened up another dimension of my journey. Since that day, I have explored more and I've loved the new discoveries of pleasure, enrichment and fulfilment I have experienced along the way, beyond the words I have expressed here.

I know kink isn't for everyone and there are parts certainly not for me, but there are elements I can't wait to explore more. It's a whole new world and I am so glad I have found it. For my 40th birthday, I treated myself to the most phenomenal rope photo shoot, where I was tied up in lots of different ropes and suspended naked from the ceiling. The pictures are amazing and it was so nice to explore kink in a different way - I am so having another photoshoot soon. This may spark some intrigue in you and you may start to dabble a little bit in the possibilities as I have not even scratched the edges here.

How can you surrender to your truth? No holding back. You can have everything, feel all the depths of pleasure if you are open to receive it.

Connection Exercises:

1) What is your relationship with pleasure?

Think about your life at the moment. Grab your journal and explore some of the questions below. You don't have to do them all at once, pick one or two and do some free writing.

- What activities/things/experiences bring you pleasure?
- What kind of pleasure are you open to and feels easier to receive?

- Where do you feel pleasure in your body?
- What's in the way of you experiencing more pleasure?
- What thoughts or emotions do you feel when you experience or stop yourself from receiving pleasure? Shame? Gratitude?

Afterwards, feel free to check in using the five steps of EAM to release any resistance to receiving all the pleasure into your life.

2) Take a Goddess Bath or Shower

When was the last time you had a lush bath, one where you felt like you were bathing in sacred water? I would love you to treat yourself to a beautiful goddess bath. If you don't have a bath, you can experience something similar in the shower. Here are some items I would recommend to make it super special and to feel all the pleasure for yourself:

- Candles
- Epsom / Himalayan salts
- Natural bath bomb or some fresh flowers
- Coconut oil
- Shower mitt / sponge
- Herbal Tea
- Facemask
- Nice fruit to snack on
- Essential oils
- Body oil for afterwards

Run quite a deep bath with lovely warm water, light the candles, dim the lights and get yourself a lovely cup of tea (you may be thinking wine would be nice but alcohol actually numbs the senses, I want you to experience everything!)

When you add your special bits to the water, set the intention to relax and receive the beauty of this experience. Send love and gratitude to what these beautiful products will bring to you.

Once in the bath, grab your sponge and start with closing your eyes and taking a breath. Connect with the five senses and open yourself up to experiencing this time for you. Wash and caress every part of your body and give love to yourself in this beautifully nourishing way.

3) Pussy Connection

For this exercise, I would like you to connect with your pussy through touch - this can be over your clothes or skin to skin, whatever feels most comfortable to you. Stroke her or place your warm hands on her. Really feel in to what she is yearning for - then say these words:

You are so beautiful, I love you. Thank You

Take a few deep breaths and repeat this 5-10 times. You may feel silly doing this but the more you say it, the more you will feel your pussy respond. This is lovely to do each morning or evening and take a few minutes. The more you connect, the more she will light up and be full of yummy pleasure and it's a lovely way to deepen the connection with this sacred part of you. It can be a real energy booster - how did it feel for you?

4) Connected Self Pleasure

If the word self-pleasure makes you feel uncomfortable, take this next exercise slowly. If you know you are in deep resistance, you can always do some releasing before you begin with some pussy and heart breaths and some EAM, with a powerful step 5 to get you ready for this self-pleasure ritual.

- Set the scene, get yourself comfy where you will feel relaxed.
- I invite you to spend some time with your body with the intention of pleasure, with no expectation or end goal, like reaching orgasm. Sometimes this can make you disconnect with what is going on in your body. Use this time to explore all of your body and get a sense of what feels nice for you.
- Start by connecting to all of your body and then spend some time listening to the part of you that is asking for more pleasure. This is not necessarily intimate areas; it's whatever feels good for you, this is your body and your pleasure.... What can you allow yourself to receive?
- If your pussy is asking to be explored or you want to but you're scared, ask her 'how do you want to be touched?' Get yourself some oil, feel the lips between your fingers and how it feels to slide over the contours of her. How is she receiving this? Do you notice her change and her lips start to change colour or size? Does she want more of this or something different? Explore all of your body, all of her. No need to rush, this is your time to explore and connect to pleasure.
- Remember throughout the whole practice, to breathe,

make sound and move your body so the energy can move through you.

- If any resistance arises, you can also try releasing with EAM whilst you are self-pleasuring. It can be extremely powerful whilst connecting with your hara energy.
- Spend some time afterwards checking in on how it felt for you.

CONSCIOUS CONNECTION WITH OTHERS

So at this stage in the book, if you've done some of the exercises, you'll be connecting more deeply to your truth, and the way you show up and connect with others is integral to this. Is it coming from a place of love and are you showing up in your truth in your relationships?

Conscious relating is about being you and not hiding the parts of yourself you think will affect how someone else loves you. It also means accepting there is no such thing as being perfect and not expecting someone else to change for you. I never even knew conscious relating was a thing and it's been a game changer in my relationship, especially over the last four years, as I have been navigating this crazy journey which has meant my relationship has changed quite significantly. Our relationship is far from perfect. It's evolving all the time and we both have our own stuff, but we take responsibility for it and that makes a huge difference. Sometimes this means navigating some huge waves that life has thrown at us and other times, it's calm and peaceful.

Conflict in a relationship is never nice and can leave you feeling rubbish but as hard as it may be to hear, when you have conflict, it is always a reflection of you. ALWAYS. It's easier to blame someone else when arguments or conflict comes up but the truth is, it's normally an indication you are missing something within yourself or are finding it hard to know or communicate what you need. It could also be triggering something from a past relationship. Let me give you an example; if you feel someone isn't showing enough love towards you, is there a reason you are not feeling this love? Are you resisting it in some way? Do you feel worthy of their love? How much do you love yourself?

On my EAM journey, I was introduced to the Relationship Triangle, also known as the Karpman Drama Triangle. This helps you understand the situations of 'drama' you can find yourself in when relating. Once you are aware of these patterns, it can help you navigate how you communicate with your loved ones in a more conscious way.

When you are in the drama triangle, no one is taking responsibility for the way they are acting, thinking or what they are saying, and so resistant energy is created. The more this happens, the more disconnected you can become from your true, authentic self.

You know what it's like when you have an argument and you say things you don't mean or blame each other for how you are feeling and it's all said in the heat of the moment? Well, this is drama and once you are aware you are entering into it, you can step outside of it and get yourself in alignment. Below is an explanation of the three roles within the triangle and although you may recognise one that you tend to default to more regularly, you can move around these depending on the situation and who you are with.

The Pusher

The pusher likes to be in control and wants to be right all the time. They want everyone around them to live by their rules and if they don't, they can be very critical, angry and authoritative. They push their thoughts and feelings and intentions on to someone else and expect others to abide by their rules and if they don't, they make sure the person knows they are not happy about it.

The Puller

The puller is the one being attacked by the pusher and feels victimised and helpless. They like to be looked after, lack in self-confidence and want others to feel sorry for them. They feel that it's so hard being them and that's why they feel so bad.

They don't take responsibility for anything. They think they are helpless and unable to resolve their own problems. They feel powerless, ashamed, unable to make decisions or see good in anything. If they have no drama going on, they will seek out the pusher and create some and

lean to the protector/rescuer to save the day.

The Protector

The protector is the nice guy and they tend to be connected to the puller, always going in to save the day. They feel needed, important and in charge. It works sometimes but the rescuer gets fed up with doing it all the time and then starts doing things out of guilt and comes from a place of fear, not love. They keep the puller dependent on them but if the puller changes and asks them to back off because they are not needed, they can quite easily step into the pusher role and say things like "after everything I have done for you, you treat me like this."

I had no idea I was a protector, so when I was introduced to the drama triangle, I realised I had been in protector energy most of my life and this was my default for sure. It goes back to the day on the kitchen floor when I decided I would become mum. That scenario then played out throughout my entire life, constantly trying to protect everyone I was around.

I remember doing it with one of my best friends too. Subconsciously I was always looking for ways to save the day and send Kerry to the rescue and they got used to me being there too. I was there through all the key events in their life and loved it... but without knowing, I think I loved to be needed and subconsciously did it because I wanted them to love me. I thought I needed to be in a place of service so they would want to spend time with me. It's all I knew and I thought when others needed me, it made me a good person. I needed that validation from others.

So do you recognise yourself in any of these roles? Don't forget you can move between all of them and the thing that keeps you in alignment is understanding when it happens. Then you can step out of it.

Where is the drama playing out in your world?

Exploring the Love Languages

This is a powerful work by Gary Chapman and the principle is simple; we all communicate love differently. This had a significant impact on how I related with Mark. It helped me to understand how I wanted another being to show love to me and what made me feel love. It also made me understand why so many relationships fail and why there can be so much tension, with all this drama and misunderstanding, on how human's experience love with each other. How did I go my entire life without knowing about these? It would have made relating so much easier.

The five love languages that he describes are following:

- Physical Touch
- Acts of Service
- Words of Affirmation
- Gifts
- Quality time

Gary Chapman explains we all think of love in a different way. An act of love for one person, may mean nothing to someone else, so it's important we understand what love means for one another. It was a real light bulb moment when I realised myself and my Mark were wired completely different.

I remember when I first got together with him, I used to get so upset when he wrote a card and put 'To Kerry, Love Mark'. No words, nothing! I write essays in my cards and I am all about the words, but he had no idea. He would clean the house and put the bins out and tell me with a huge smile on his face expecting me to be over the moon. I was grateful of course but

I would much prefer him to give me a huge hug, stroke my hair and honour me with beautiful words in a card.

Those things make me feel warm inside and touch my heart. Putting the bins out did not float my boat and has no impact on me where love is concerned. Everyone is different, so you can't expect to love the same things.

Mark's love language is Acts of Service. OMG, it made so much sense when I found out. When I ironed his shirts one day, he smiled from ear to ear like I'd done something amazing for him as that's the kind of love that touches his heart. What this means is when you relate with someone and understand their love language, you can meet them in love and do the things they enjoy.

It's great to understand this about everyone you relate with and it's not just a romantic thing. I know my mum is the same as me and why one year, when I got her a mother's day card with only a few words, she was a bit upset. My mum loves all the words like me, so I spend ages now finding the best card with the most gorgeous words and I add to them too. My mum takes the time to read every word and always has a huge beam on her face and it's worth all the extra effort I go to.

Are you feeling intrigued now to find out what yours is and everyone you relate with?

It always comes back to LOVE …

How do you like to be touched?

Conscious touch with others

I have learnt so much about conscious touch in the last few years, gaining an understanding of what I desired when it comes to touch but also how to receive it more deeply. It's also changed how I give touch to others and I'm a lot more present in the moment, which has added to the experience. I know a lot of the time, without even knowing it, I didn't feel worthy of love and to fully express my needs and desires out loud to someone else. Safety played a huge part too. When I felt safe, I gave myself permission to let go with another.

One of the biggest questions I have from clients is what if I don't know what I want? I never did, but the more I dropped into my body and gave myself permission to feel, I was able to listen more to what felt good and what didn't.

When you have this understanding, you can create your own boundaries around touch and define what is a yes and what is no for you. Creating a space with consent and boundaries in place means you are more likely to have your needs met and are able to drop into receiving it more deeply too.

Conscious sensual touch doesn't need to be with a romantic partner; it can also be with your friends or relatives. Think of when you hug someone or they hug you, do you pull away quickly or do you feel the hug deeply? Next time you give or receive a hug, spend a little longer and take a few more breaths than what you are used too. It feels awkward at first but in time, you'll start to feel the deliciousness of dropping more deeply to the hug. Try it and you will know exactly what I mean.

The role of the giver or the receiver

In romantic relationships, it's easy to do what you've always done or wrap yourself up in what you are supposed to be doing rather than saying what you want. A habit of rushing is a common one, going straight for the area of the body you know will excite your partner. The body has so many erogenous zones that are often missed, places like the insides of the arms and legs, your back, your bum, the side of your beautiful curves, the backs of your ears. Taking your time, being present with the receiver and how they respond can go a long way to deepening the connection between you. There is so much more pleasure to be experienced when you don't rush the process, when you allow yourself to feel and let your body slowly awaken – are you excited to explore this?

One powerful way to enhance the connection is for you to take a role as the giver or the receiver, as dancing between them can then lead to you feeling unfulfilled in both roles. If one of you is always the giver, it's likely there is some resistance to receiving love and if you are the receiver, you may have never considered what it would be like to switch roles. A couple of years ago, I did a tantric experience for a couple who had been married 30 years. The husband had always been the giver as he loved to give and the wife had always happily received. It worked for them and they had a beautiful relationship. In the experience, they both played the role of giver and receiver and were blown away by the experience. It was so moving to witness them both drop into these new roles and experience the pleasure of seeing their beloveds receive in a new way. I had the most gorgeous testimonial '*we are looking forward to experiencing a newfound love, connection and excitement in our relationship*'.

Defining the roles, you are playing adds a new dimension to the connection so you can embody it. When you switch between giver and receiver, the idea that you 'should' switch roles can feel distracting and stop you from being present in the moment. When present, you can connect to what you are feeling, moment by moment, clearing any thoughts of what you felt before, what you may feel later, but focussing what is happening in that VERY moment.

Who is the touch for?

The Wheel of Consent is a huge piece of work by Betty Martin and explores the dynamics that arise when you give and receive to another through touch. It explores consent and asking for what you want. I am still exploring the depths of this work but wanted to share these questions here and raise awareness of this phenomenal work as it has transformed the way I engage with others through touch.

The following questions helped me clarify my role in touch connections but also to understand what I wanted:

- How do you want to be touched?
- How do you want me to touch you?
- Who is the touch for?

These questions are so powerful and they open up a deeper enquiry around not only how you communicate what you desire, but also how it feels to meet someone else's needs.

The wheel of consent is divided into four quadrants:

- Serve – You do x for someone to give them pleasure.

- Allow – You allow someone to do x to you to give them pleasure.
- Take – You do x for someone to get pleasure for yourself.
- Accept – you accept x from someone to get pleasure for yourself.

Many people like the simplicity of the quadrants as you know where you are and you can focus on one pleasure at a time: the pleasure of taking what you want, the pleasure of somebody using you to turn themselves on, the pleasure of serving somebody or the pleasure of someone focusing all their attention on getting you excited.

However, the question of asking or acknowledging what you want may bring up all sorts of emotions in you, especially if this is something you have never been asked and you have no clue where to start.

The wheel of consent is such an expansive tool and can be applied to a lot of situations. I would recommend you go and check out Betty Martin's work, her free resources are amazing and she has a great 3-minute game that you can do to practice these dynamics too.

My journey into receiving love only started three years ago. Before then, I had no self-awareness of how I was feeling and what my mind and body needed. I still have days when things crop up but now I have the tools to embody what is arising in me so I drop more fully into my body. I remember the first time I let myself receive love and surrender into what was coming up for me. I was training in tantric massage and I was going to receive an honouring of my body.

Letting others love me is a sign of how much I love myself

I worked with a beautiful Shiva who I had only met that day. I stood before him dressed in a sarong waiting for the ritual to begin. He began with honouring my body with an energetic circle of love, he spoke beautiful words to me as he took me in, he caressed my skin, bowed to my feet and honoured every part of my being. I stood before him and I cried my eyes out. I had never been touched with such love, tenderness and care, and with no intention but to honour every part of me. I had never allowed myself to receive, yet here I was, surrendering to it all. It was so beautiful and I felt it deep into my heart. For me, this was about feeling loved, accepting love and feeling safe. My reaction totally surprised me; this was such a simple exercise yet had such a powerful effect on me and makes me alive with goosebumps as I type. I will never forget the bond I shared with the beautiful soul I had just met. I felt so radiant, I was submerged deep into my feminine energy and it felt so wonderful. From that day, I made a promise to myself, I would honour myself always, always speak up and create safe spaces for myself to fully let go and to receive love. Giving to others was my default but to receive was so powerful and I knew I was now worthy enough. I was beautiful.

So let's start to explore your relationships:

Connection Exercises:

1) Exploring your relationships

Looking at the main relationships in your life, spend some time journaling on the following questions:

- How do I feel empowered or disempowered in this relationship?
- Do I show up as me in the relationship?
- Do I find it easy to communicate what I desire?
- What do I love about the relationship?
- What areas do I find challenging?
- What ways would I like the relationship to be transformed?

2) Sending love in conflict

This is a beautiful exercise to connect to love, even when your entire being may want to do the opposite. When someone is in projection mode and you feel hurt or you are not being met in love, rather than go into the drama triangle, connect to love and send it their way. I believe it always comes back to love. Always. If you can't bring yourself to engage in love, know with intention and closing your eyes and connecting to their heart, you can send it without saying a word. It really works.

It always amazes me to see how quickly the feeling of irritation and awkwardness disappears, but we are all energy so it totally makes sense.

You can use this practice across all areas of your life and so, whenever you feel the absence of love in a situation, use this practice to give LOVE, to connect you in unity on this level of awareness from one soul to another. It can be applied to all relationships in your life.

LIVING YOUR TRUTH

If you've got this far into the book, I would love you to give yourself a HUGE hug. I love that you have given yourself the time to grow and explore the depths of your soul and, if you've been doing the exercises, you'll know it's not always easy to connect to the parts of yourself you may have hidden for a long time.

Every time you lean in and surrender to the truth of who you are and let yourself embody it, you raise your vibration as you are connecting to the highest vibration energy of all – love.

When you choose love, you raise your vibration and every single area of your life is impacted. This is the reason I lean in to my truth every single day.

I would love you to remember that the journey never stops. I used to think there came an end point when you were fixed. I was limiting myself with this because why would I ever want it to stop? Life is all about learning and expanding and that feels so exciting for me.

*I am ready
to step into
my power
and be me*

Being happy means accepting things will arise that you have no control over and can completely knock you off your perch. However, the wonderful thing with energy is, even if you don't decide to explore this further, you have some practices here that will continue the journey for you and can transform your energy in an instant.

When your light is dimmed in some way, you have a choice:

- Do I want to stay here, sit with it and surrender to what I am feeling? Is there a lesson for me to learn here?
- Do I want to do some energy work and get myself out of the funk I am in and transform my energy?

It ALWAYS comes down to choice - to stay with your light dimmed or step into your truth, to your power and SHINE.

Here are my favourite practises I do every day to deepen the connection to myself:

Spend time in silence

From someone that never stopped and ran away from silence, I find time for silence every day. It doesn't have to be long, just a few minutes a day to check in with yourself and see how you are and what you need. You can also spend this time to think nothing at all and rest your mind. It is so powerful in its simplicity.

I surrender
to my truth

Say hello to your pussy

I connect and talk to my pussy every day and she has a lot to say to me too. Like I've already explained, if you decide when you put this book down to never give her another thought, she will go to sleep because it's energy and she likes to be spoken too. Every day I invite you to say hello to her and you can do this energetically, with intention, or physically by placing your hand over your vulva or by enjoying some self-pleasure. The more you talk to her, the more she will respond and the more you will connect to her delicious power. If you take anything from this book, know there is always more to be experienced, even if this is the beginning of the conversation.

Continue to ignite your sexual power

Your sexual power is so powerful, you can use it for everything. The more you speak to your pussy, the more alive she will become. When you start to feel the activation of your sexual energy, use it and let it be unleashed across your whole entire body. The more you practice the embodiment of this, the more you will feel. Don't forget to go and experience my bonus sexual energy activation on (www.kerryosullivan.co.uk/book) and there is more information on The Goddess Awakening® too, which delves even deeper into the magic of turning yourself on.

Continually lean into what feels uncomfortable

This takes practice, knowing and accepting stuff will come up all the time for you. But the more you embrace all you are and don't run away, the more you will learn and expand into the truth of who you are.

I lean into the uncomfortable

I've navigated some challenging times this year, with things that were completely out of my control, but I trust it's all part of the journey and all part of my expansion and growth of the person I am becoming and it helps me to lean in.

These uncomfortable thoughts and feelings come up as it's your energy's way of letting you know, these patterns are still there. They come up as they are ready to be set free. The more you set yourself free, the higher you rise and the more you surrender into your truth and to the version that is ready to shine in this world.

Make yourself a soundtrack that lifts your spirits

I have a playlist which is my go to when I know I need an energetic boost. Music does something amazing for me and the more embodied I have become, the more I feel and it feels so good! I have all sorts in there: crazy tracks that get me jumping around, slow and sensual if I want to connect to pussy and get my sexy on.

I also have songs that give me the incentive to get into emotions like rage and clear resistance in my body, or songs to relax to. I love the music loud in my ears and I'd recommend a wireless headset so you can let go and shake your booty. Go check out my bonuses for some of my favourite songs (www.kerryosullivan.co.uk/book).

So let's spend some time now to reflect on your journey so far:

Connection Exercises:

1) Reflection

This is a nice journaling exercise for you to reflect on your journey and to celebrate and acknowledge some of the areas you would like to focus on going forward. Take some time to sit down somewhere nice and chilled with your journal.

- Before you begin, spend a few moments connecting to your heart and take some beautiful heart breaths here.
- What has been your biggest lesson?
- Was there anything that surprised you?
- What does it feel like to be in your goddess power?
- Reflect on the times when you have you noticed this power play out in your life. How did it feel, energetically?
- Are there some areas you would like to go over and do some more work on?

I connect with my pussy every day

2) Celebrate YOU and embody all you are

I invite you to surrender into your truth and celebrate with a beautiful embodied dance. By now, you know yourself, how you like to be touched and how you love to be pleasured – let's bring all this together and have a beautiful sexy sensual goddess dance – time to shake your booty.

There is no such thing as not being able to dance; music can take you to a delicious place for you to embody all of you. If you find it hard, close your eyes, feel into your body and put you hand on your heart and pussy and allow yourself to connect to the music and connect to you. I have some great tunes on the playlist I've put together if you want some inspiration (www.kerryosullivan.co.uk/book).

I love all of me

MY INVITATION IF YOU'D LIKE TO CONTINUE THE JOURNEY

It's never the end… this is only the beginning…

Write me a letter

I love nothing better than to hear about other's journeys. The work I do in the world totally lights up my world and I love to receive letters in the post. If you feel called, I would love to hear about your journey to Surrender to Your Truth – You can write to me here: PO BOX 1414, Maidstone, United Kingdom, ME14 9YY

Book bonuses

If you'd like to get a download of my gorgeous chakra meditation, pussy activation and a fabulous Spotify playlist – sign up here - www.kerryosullivan.co.uk/book

Working with me 121

I tailor all my 121 packages to you. If you are interested to know more about my 121 coaching or tantric embodiment sessions go to www.kerryosullivan.co.uk or email me at info@kerryosullivan.co.uk

Join The Goddess Awakening®

The Goddess Awakening is my group coaching programme to awaken the goddess within you, to connect to your inner beauty, learning to embrace all of you and allowing more love and pleasure into your life. The journey goes into more depth than this book with weekly accountability calls to support you on your own journey, as well as embodiment practices to embody the goddess and the truth of who you are. You can find out more here - https://www.kerryosullivan.co.uk/thegoddessawakening

Deepening Intimacy for Couples

Deepening Intimacy programme is a beautiful 6-week journey to deepen the love between you. Explore and understand each other in new ways and learn quick and effective energy practices to use every day to clear anything that is stopping you showing up in your truth. You can find out more here - https://www.kerryosullivan.co.uk/deepeningintimacy

KIND WORDS FROM MY CLIENTS

I have been on my own spiritual and personal development journey for over 25 years and supporting others professionally worldwide for over a decade in recognising themselves as spiritual beings and creating deep transformations. A few years ago, I became very interested in Tantra and falling in love with myself after I split from my ex and became a single mother. I first met Kerry at EAM events a few years ago when I was on their 10-month journey and loved her bubbly, friendly nature then.

On seeing her free masterclass, I joined, as I'm always open to learning and growing, plus I loved the tantric aspect however, I was amazed to recognise I didn't actually listen to my body! I knew I was joining Kerry on her 12-week program after that first free masterclass and signed up immediately!

I felt a deep connection to Kerry on a soul level however, as it came closer to starting the course, I became a little resistant! I absolutely love Kerry's gorgeous authentic energy and how she holds space for people. As someone who helps and heals others,

I find it incredibly hard to be vulnerable myself. On this course, I was able to open up and admit that. I loved how Kerry could call me out on my shit where others have missed that before! I loved the embodiment sessions and the Q&A calls each week. These were deep and powerful. It was so lovely connecting with the other goddesses and deepening the connection with myself. Kerry is so down to earth and lovely, yet powerful in how she empowers you. I must admit, if this had been another online course I would have dropped off as I had huge resistance come up during it, but having my 121 with Kerry was a huge game changer for me! It was the first time I truly felt and embodied what was deep inside of me. I have come away with new ways of connecting with myself plus helping others in the work I do in the world. I also had the pleasure of a tantric massage with Kerry. This was profound... It was nourishing, gentle and exquisite. It allowed me to go deep into receiving pleasure and be totally vulnerable. I highly recommend the Goddess Awakening, the tantric massage and Kerry. Thank you, Gorgeous, for being you and all you are.

Sarah

Kerry is an incredibly inspiring, beautiful soul on this planet. Her Goddess Awakening journey is life changing in the best possible way, and I feel this is only the beginning for anyone that embarks on this journey. It is empowering, unravelling and unlearning what no longer serves you, so that you can rebuild, relearn and reconnect with your true feminine nature and use this to create a life you love, enriched with pleasure, joy and sensuality.

This felt like a frightening step to take to begin with because I knew this journey would challenge deeply held beliefs, habits and behaviours that were not supporting me! I felt restrained by time at first, yet every time I consciously made the time, my mind body and soul breathed an enormous sigh of relief and gratitude and I expanded and opened a little more, feeling freer and enjoying more of my day and my life. I realised time was a convenient avoidance tactic and now I make the time EVERY DAY, even if just a small amount, to connect with my body, my heart, my soul.

Since starting this journey, I can see how the more I pause and feel into my body, instead of listening to the mindless head chatter, the clearer my inner knowing is. The Goddess Awakening has taught me to FEEL yes and no answers in my body, instead of getting lost thinking about them in my head. I'm learning to tell the difference between 'head stuff', what's true and what I really want. I'm learning to feel pleasure and sensuality again. I am learning to truly love and embrace all that I am, have been and all that I am becoming. This journey is truly a gift. Never have I felt so held, safe, witnessed, honoured, guided and held accountable, as I have on this journey, with Kerry - sharing her incredible experience, wisdom and knowledge from her epic heart, and also by the other beautiful women in the group.

Carli

What I received from The Goddess Awakening Course was beyond my ability to understand at the outset. My Soul knew what it needed but my mind did not. It was only after the course had finished and I reflected, that I realised I had received the care, love, guidance, wisdom and knowledge about my body and my sexuality that had been completely lacking from my childhood. I had been truly heard, understood and seen for the first time. I had unconsciously been searching for this but never found a safe, non-judgemental environment or a mentor I could trust to receive this from. It felt as if my younger self had been given back the missing pieces that she had unknowingly been searching for - that she had given away to keep herself safe. I felt I had been given permission and felt safe to be that lost, lonely, confused frightened little me and be received with love, nurturing and understanding. When the course ended, I felt more complete, like I had grown up and become a woman for the first time. I felt I had permission to be me, warts and all. Kerry's non-judgemental, all-embracing, unconditional love and unique energy revealed wounds I didn't know I had and empowered me to heal them very quickly. The practices I learned on this course are transformative, easy to apply and I use many of them every day. If you are considering signing up for this course and need a big why to do so, know that it may well be invisible and could be the key that can unlock and expand a sacred place inside that has the capacity to give and receive love in ways never before, and in ways never thought possible – well it did for me. I have gone beyond what I thought was possible for me to experience and I've only just started! Thank you, Kerry, for giving me back to myself and all my little mes too. You are a gift to this world and to everyone whose life you touch.

Louise

I first met Kerry on a weekend EAM course, which was all new to me. I didn't really understand much about energy alignment or Tantra.

However, as soon as I saw Kerry doing her magic, I was completely blown away by her and how my whole being responded to her work. From the aliveness in my body and what I was experiencing, I knew from that very moment she had something very special and I wanted to work with her. The love, power and natural gift she has for making you feel loved, safe, and alive goes beyond words.

Of course, I started to hesitate - Am I worthy? Do I deserve to be investing in myself? - and feeling a sense of guilt to do that.

Everyone and everything were more important, as I had always put everyone else's needs first - just like most, I guess.

My poor inner child hadn't received any love and had been suppressed, feeling lonely and unloved.

I made every excuse and just couldn't justify spending the time and money on myself. If it had been for someone else in my family, I would have been the first to say 'YES, do it'.

Wow, how wrong was I? After taking the leap and finally deciding to invest in myself, it wasn't just investing in me it was investing in every one of my family members too. They felt this new aliveness embodied and powerful positive love inside of me which in turn, had an impact on them.

How much I regret not saying yes before and taking so long to decide.

I did feel nervous at the start because I didn't have much self-confidence. Kerry and the other beautiful goddesses soon changed that.

It's a beautiful safe space and everyone supports, loves, and holds one another.

We journey together like true Sisterhood you feel it's safe to be vulnerable and speak your own truth, taking down the mask.

It's just so beautiful. There are tears, laughter and lots of love.

On our first call, I cried and cried. I hadn't been able to cry for a long time, even though many times I'd wanted to.

I now know it was my inner child saying thank you to me for eventually showing her the love she truly deserves.

This was just the beginning of a life changing journey.

I would feel so excited, from one week to the next, to learn more.

The embodiment sessions are something else. So deeply powerful it's actually breath-taking. Kerry teaches you life changing tools that I will be living by and using for the rest of my life.

I will be eternally grateful to Kerry. She's completely transformed my life and taught me so much.

She's honestly one special soul queen goddess. My deep love and admiration for her and her teachings is unimaginable.

From one goddess to another, sending love. And if you are considering doing the Goddess Awakening, just say YES because you won't regret it.

Lisa

The Goddess Awakening came at just the right time in my journey. I've done so much personal change work, mostly with NLP and hypnotic language, which has created some profound shifts. Yet there was this missing piece: the connection to my powerful sexual energy, that I'd ignored for too long. You've given such a beautiful container to do that work, and have so much knowledge and experience. I just can't thank you enough for the Goddess Awakening; it's such an intense and healing journey. Wow. I knew I had some stuff to shift in me around intimacy, and some healing to do. How Kerry turned up for the calls was so perfect. Her honesty and the work we did together really helped me through a very intense shift in my life. A few months after we finished, I started a new relationship, and have been experiencing such beautiful levels of emotional honesty and intimacy. Really though, the most profound intimacy is that which I now feel with myself. This opened me up to that, which is just gorgeous.

Claire

The Goddess Awakening. My experience is as an NLP coach, which gives you the ability to always try to fix things, create change, forward think and goal set, which are amazing qualities and learnings, but all very masculine. The Goddess Awakening is the feminine. Feeling the now, embodiment and exploration of my feminine essence and divine birth right power. Not structured and disciplined. But flowy and yummy. I Loved it and learnt so much about myself. I now feel I have balance. So, thanks, Kerry.

Nicola

The Goddess Awakening Journey really enabled me to step out of the shadow I'd created around myself. I've gained practical tools that I can use every day to check in with myself and get rid of unhelpful feelings and the way these manifest physically and mentally.

I've also gained clarity about what I want out of my future, and I honestly think I wouldn't have made the time and space to do this if I hadn't joined the course.

There's a lot to get through and a healthy level of challenge, which I needed; all within a lovely supportive community held together beautifully by Kerry. I could've easily spent the money on material possessions but I've invested it in me and it's the best gift I could've given myself! If you're wondering whether to join the next course and whether it's any good, I don't hesitate to say: GO FOR IT.

Shelley

Wow, just wow! I am so grateful to Kerry for the past 12 weeks and I am grateful to myself that I loved myself enough and wanted to improve myself enough to sign up for this life changing course. I am full of gratitude. I have thoroughly loved every minute, even those when Kerry has given me a loving kick up the arse! My biggest success story from the past 12 weeks is how I no longer feel the need to look outside of myself to have opinions, belief, love and feelings. Prior to this course, I spent so much time worrying about what others thought and (without realising) I allowed myself to be numb to what I wanted, needed or indeed felt. Not now. Now I have found my inner goddess and I know that the only person's opinion that matters and whose feelings I listen to are my own! I love me! Genuinely, I am so much better at listening to myself and recognising what I need after this course, because I know now that I deserve love and that starts with loving me!

Kerry has strengthened my understanding and use of EAM, but alongside this, I am now using more tantric embodiment exercises to really feel into my body to see what lessons and messages I need to hear and know. I am standing in my power more and creating healthier boundaries, which are in my greatest interest. I am listening to my inner goddess – and she certainly knows what is best for me. The 'body' work weeks were challenging and there was more resistance with some than others! However, Kerry was always there for support and guidance and I have come out of it loving my body – every single part of it! I have new practises for self-pleasure, in every meaning of the pleasure word, and I am beginning to develop an understanding on what actually feels pleasurable for me. It's great, I am learning to love myself at a deeper level and all thanks to Kerry and the practises she shared with us and taught us. But also, I again thank myself for taking responsibility to practise what Kerry had taught and to address things as they came up. You do have to put the work in and it is worth every minute!

My inner shadow self was the biggest challenge for me and I spent a lot of time learning to love those parts of me that aren't easy to love. It was funny how the universe kept bringing people and situations into my life in line with what we were working on in the group, emphasising my shadow. It enabled me to see when I had worked and released, and when I needed more work! My shadow self is still an aspect of me I need to work on daily, but I have learnt to love what I am being shown and to ask my body what the lesson is I need to learn.

It is an ongoing process to be a total goddess and to stay in your power, but I know I have the skills to do this and do it with pride, thanks to the past empowering 12 weeks! I must also add what amazing friendships I made on the course and how lucky

I feel to have worked with Kerry and the other Goddesses – I feel blessed and glowing!

Penny

I completed the Goddess Awakening Journey. My main reason for doing the journey was to focus on my self-care. And it was great to identify what I was neglecting in myself (not necessarily on purpose but things I wasn't aware of).

It allowed me to tune into what I really wanted from life, who I really am and be able to step into being that person, without worrying about what others thought.

It also allowed me to bring balance into my life, identify resistances I didn't realise were there as they never came up as an issue but were really amazing to identify and clear, and it also has allowed me to be stronger in my relationship with my boyfriend.

For anyone who is worried about doing the journey, don't be. It is gentle. You have the support of Kerry and the group, and you discover so much about yourself, which allows you to be more confident and in your power.

If you are thinking about doing the course, but are a bit scared of it, then just GO FOR IT! You won't regret it.

Ceza

Kerry's Goddess Awakening Journey is just that....an Awakening to a part of YOU, deep within, that you didn't even realise was there......

It's beautiful, Supportive and truly Authentic. The Embodiment work and Activations are inspiring and when you fully open to the process, it allows you to connect to the TRUE INNER YOU!

It's an exciting and a beautiful unfolding - Say YES to YOU. Say YES to the Power within YOU. Say YES to the Greatness within YOU - Allow Yourself to Live

The one word I had at the end of the 12 weeks was "Alive" and having spent most of my life in Survival mode, this really was an Amazing Outcome

So much Love and Gratitude xxxxxxxxx 🧡🧡🧡🧡🧡🧡🧡

Aine

I am so grateful to have had Kerry hold such a beautiful space for me on the Goddess Awakening Journey. What a powerful 12 weeks that was. Her methods provided for deep healing, deep connection with myself, and for a nurturing transformation.

The biggest transformation occurred during her embodiment sessions and tantric breathing exercises. These sessions were amazing, being held in such a safe, warm, nurturing and in a connected Sisterhood space. I now listen and connect to my body so much more, creating healthy boundaries for myself and putting my self-care and self-love as my top priority.

During the journey there were a number of inner shadows and triggers that came up. Kerry was always there to support, provide advice, direction, helping me transform and heal, returning myself back to a place of love.

Speaking of being in a place of love, because I loved the Goddess Awakening journey so much I have decided to continue my journey with Kerry, this time for the "Deepening Intimacy" journey with my Husband. Let the connections, love, fun and laughter continue!

Yvonne

I have worked with energy and EAM for several years now and actually felt like I was in a relatively good place prior to commencing the programme.

I first met Kerry on an online, expand your love EAM weekend, with Yvette Taylor. I was enchanted and captured with Kerry's energy and the session she did. It really resonated with me and so I booked a 121 session with her.

The impact of the 121 made me want more. I realised this was what I had truly been looking for to release me from my past limitations, repeat patterns of behaviour and truly connect with my sexual energy. This was something which I felt had been a little absent for a few years and had attributed this to where I was in my life.

I'm not going to lie, I had a fair bit of resistance to signing up for the course. I had been doing a lot of work around financial abundance and clearing previous spending. Paying for a course seemed counterproductive to what I was working towards.

How wrong I was.

Whilst I thought I already had self-care/ self-love practices in place to nurture myself, I quickly realised that this could be on a much deeper level and I could connect to my body and manifest like never before.

I shifted issues from past relationships, became more attuned and able to listen to my body, what she needs and wants and further develop my intuitive self.

I journeyed through the embodiment work and felt the shifts, some having a greater impact and more powerful than others, but all leading me to a place of a more empowered and sure self; sometimes feeling a deep peacefulness and contentment and at other times, I can take on the world and win attitude, with an abundance of vitality and energy

I loved meeting the other Goddesses and journeying with them. It was amazing to see the synchronicity between us and how much we complimented and reflected each other's moods and feelings.

This journey is obviously different for each individual but what I know for sure is that you will feel loved, supported and held by Kerry and the other Goddesses, in a safe place to release emotions.

To anyone considering signing up ... DO IT! You won't regret this.

Shelley

What a lovely journey! Eventually saying YES to myself! I joined this wonderful course as I really wanted to connect to myself at a much deeper level and allow myself that time to work on different areas.

Honestly, it has truly opened my eyes and highlighted that everything you really require is all inside of you - you just have to go within, do the work and keep practising.

The beauty of the course is that there are 12 different areas that Kerry focuses on throughout the 12 weeks, so there is a lot of "yummy" stuff as Kerry would say!

I feel I have grown a lot over the past 12 weeks. My sense of awareness has been massively heightened and this really serves me. I know when to take a step back, slow down and listen to what my mind and body wants. Another thing which has been massive for me is that I have allowed myself to be vulnerable, to be seen and be me.

I have learnt that the reason I originally craved that external validation was because I was not giving myself the love first and even though this is a work in progress, I now have the tools and methods in place.

There were things that showed up throughout that were uncomfortable, however, you know what? That's also amazing at the same time because it highlights that you are a human and we all have parts that require more work than others. At the same time, I am learning to love all of me.

Kerry is a beautiful person and I felt a great connection with her from the start. It is clear she has a deep passion and love for what she does and she is with you every step of the way. The support you get throughout this course is amazing.

I feel like I have stepped into my power and I have a new found love and appreciation for myself. I do feel awakened. I feel new doors are opening for me and it's exciting!

I am so very grateful to have Kerry in my life and I have formed amazing friendships for life with her and the other Goddess on the course.

You owe it to yourself to say yes to yourself!

Big love ❤ ❤

Emma

As it's the last day of this decade, I have been reflecting on my year. The last quarter, I spent an amazing time with some lovely women on the Goddess journey. What did it do for me? Well, as a completely shy person, I was scared of what it was going to ask me to do. But my fears were unfounded. The journey is very gentle and actually requires only short amounts of time each morning and I suspect, as the new year dawns, we can all do with changing up our morning routine!

The worksheets can be completed at your leisure. I found my time was on a Monday morning. This worked well for me! And it really did set me up for the rest 'of the week. Kerry works with you in a very gentle and caring way. You are in safe hands every step of the way.

So what did I gain? Well, I gained the perspective that I am always able to be in my goddess power whenever I want. It does feel different. I am actually more confident in being open and honest with how I am feeling and noting that it is ok to just be, but then I am able to use the techniques learnt, when I am ready to give what comes up a kick into touch.

If you are wanting a completely new perspective for the new decade, then this course works with exactly what you need right now. Don't delay, the time is now!

Jennifer

Kerry and her Goddess Awakening program has and is changing my life.

I first experienced the magic that Kerry teaches at an EAM weekend during lockdown one. I cried my way through her session – it cracked me open, woke me up and made me realise how much of myself I had shut down, hidden, and held on to for 'safety' and 'protection'! I knew I needed to work with her, it just took me a while to take the leap!

Joining the program was a major step and release for me. Just spending that money on myself felt hugely indulgent and alien to me. Honestly, I was petrified, waves of fear and panic, that I knew deep down were a good thing. Kerry's kindness and patience helped me know I was doing the right thing and only good would come of it. I nervously joined the first call to find that we all felt the same. The tears flowed, the resistance released, and we danced to begin our journey.

Working each week with Kerry and such a beautiful group of Goddesses was an experience I will never forget. Never have I felt so safely held, so listened to, so excepted and able to bring all of myself to the table.

Kerry is such a warm and intuitive person, from the way she lets you speak until you're finished, her music choices, the timing of the subjects she covers or the things she talks about, always perfectly synchronized with the goddesses, how they feel and what is coming up for them.

The Goddess Awakening has done just that! It has woken up the connection with my body, with feelings of pleasure, acceptance, self-love. It taught me to stop and listen to myself, my inner child, the truth in my heart and what my body is wanting not my head! Most importantly it has enabled me to actually take the action needed to step into my truth and my power and be me!

My attitude to self-care has shifted to it being an essential part of me being me. I feel more confident, grounded, calmer and happier. I am loving making choices because they serve me and not because I think I should! I found returning to work much easier than last July and I feel able to be more open with my clients. They return this with increased openness too. I have found myself connecting on a deeper level with some of my friends and feeling like I am fully listening and being heard.

All of this is just the start! There is so much more for me, and I continue to use the techniques and teachings Kerry has given me each day. Kerry thank you for your kindness, support, guidance, and love during this incredible experience. Thanks to you I am excited for my future and becoming the women I would like to be. You have a special gift!

Helen

I have been fortunate enough to have had two EAM sessions with Kerry and I can honestly say that they have had a profound and very positive impact on my life.

I went into the first one not knowing what to expect or where to start. Kerry was brilliant at helping me to work through the jumble in my head and focus on what I really need help with. As I released the negative energy, I genuinely felt lighter, as though a fog of anger, frustration and indecision had been lifted. I feel positive about my career choices and am definitely happier in myself.

I want to thank Kerry for her time and enthusiasm. The sessions were challenging for me; I found myself opening up about some very personal issues, but she was so professional and treated this with respect and understanding for which I am very grateful. Thank you Kerry.

Rebecca

I had an amazing VIP day with Kerry. She is absolutely fabulous. The experience has been life changing!

Sarah

WOW. WOW. WOW....Yesterday I attended a VIP day with Kerry where I learnt about EAM Energy Alignment Method. Kerry is a very friendly, warm person, which instantly put me at ease. I was completely blown away with how instantly effective this method is and once we had finished, I was amazed at how free I felt. I felt this negative energy lift from my body. To sum up my day... AMAZING, LIFE CHANGING, TRANSFORMATIONAL.

Lynne

I just wanted to say thank you for introducing me to Tantra. I can so relate to your blog about self-pleasure - that was so me for many years, but you helped me change that last year after my Yoni massage... I feel so much more connected to my body and in love with myself for the first time ever. I am taking so much more care of all aspects of loving myself through eating well, exercise, time for me, but also knowing that it is ok for me to love myself whichever way I desire and now regularly start my day in front of the mirror naked, admiring myself and loving what I see... This, growing up, was an absolute no-no, which fuelled feelings for many years of guilt, shame, disgust. Thankfully, that has all gone, thanks to you.

My Tantra experience helped me to connect to my true authentic self for the first time. I can remember being around 11/12 years old when I started to recognise my body was changing. I can remember how I got pleasure from intimately touching myself. One day I was caught and I never lived it down. I was subjected to a huge amount of shame at that time and even later on, when I started my periods. Puberty and Sex were taboo subjects in our house. This left me with a huge amount of guilt and disgust for myself for many, many years.

Thankfully I have a loving husband who embraces all of me, but I could never do that for myself. After meeting Kerry, I immediately felt comfortable in her presence. Kerry provided me with a safe and trustworthy space where I felt accepted without any judgement. This enabled me to really embrace my Tantra experience and Yoni Massage and I never once felt like I was doing anything wrong. I felt free to truly be myself and it was so liberating. When I got emotional, Kerry held that space, which allowed me the time for myself to really let go of all the negative energy I had been carrying in my Yoni for many years.

Since that time, I embrace all aspects of loving, taking care of myself so much more. I no longer feel guilt or shame for loving myself through self-pleasure and listening to my own desires, of which I denied myself for many years as I was lead to believe it was wrong.

I can now stand in front of the mirror naked and admire my own reflection and love what I see. Thank you

Lynne

I have been on a self/personal development journey for the past nine years. Well, that is my conscious knowing of that journey. I realize now that all things I have experienced have led me to this point.

This, for me, is year of completion and letting go of 'the old' and things that no longer serve the person I am becoming and my purpose here, in this life.

Having said all that lays the foundation for WHY I sought out Kerry for the Tantric work she does.

I met Kerry at another Personal and Spiritual development training that we were both doing, over a year long period. I watched Kerry do the work on herself, open herself to discovery, healing and knowing herself from the inside out.

So, when it became clear that I needed to step into a deeper, more powerfully feminine connection with myself, I knew that Kerry was the person I trusted most to take me on a tantric Shakti Experience.

From the moment I started asking her questions about what a tantric experience was, she was understanding, professional and kind. She was clear on what to expect and also empathetic and curious about the journey I was taking. More than just asking pre-session questions, Kerry delved into how and why I had chosen Tantra to further the knowing of myself and my ability to connect to others.

The Tantric Shakti Experience with Kerry was magical and moving.

She created a safe and heart warmed space, which alleviated any concerns or reservations I had. I felt welcomed, I felt honoured, I felt loved throughout the experience. More than just in that space at that time, it was like a gift I received that has stayed with me since. It has opened me to possibilities, to love, to receiving, to allowing myself to soften and be loved.

I am a kinaesthetic person and I learn by doing and feeling. Where years of talk therapies and other spiritual modalities had only hinted at solutions and in some ways, offered lip service to the spiritual connection between my body, mind, heart and sexuality, the tantric experience took me to that place of connection and experiencing a spiritual depth to the physical like never before.

Having this experience with someone trained and compassionate enough to guide, to listen, to appreciate, to respect, to see and hear me as I am, was powerful beyond measure.

As I write this it makes me emotional, appreciative and joyful all at the same time.

Ruth

Kerry and I met at the first Tantra workshop I attended. I was incredibly nervous as I was at the beginning of my sexual exploration journey, having suffered from sexual abuse as a teenager. It seemed that Kerry instinctively sensed my fears and helped put me at ease by sharing her story, background and insights.

I then booked for a Tantra massage, which was so much more than a massage. It is more of therapeutic physical energy release as past emotional trauma that is being held by the body is healed. Kerry has taught me that my feminine sexuality is something to be celebrated and not ashamed of, and I will always be grateful that she came into my life. Thank you Kerry x

Aisling

Wow, what an experience! It was just what I needed, when I needed it.

I wasn't sure exactly what to expect but Kerry explained clearly and made me feel very comfortable in a short space of time and throughout, she was always checking what I was comfortable with.

The massage itself was beautiful and allowed me a much needed emotional release. I continued to cry after the massage had finished but I didn't feel any pressure to leave; Kerry gave me a safe space to express my emotions.

In the days that followed I felt lighter, more energised and had so much clarity.

I would 100% recommend visiting Kerry for a Tantric Massage. The benefits are amazing and plentiful.

Natalie

Thank you Kerry for the most amazing Tantra Experience. I was so excited before I went and knew it was what my body needed, but I was also anxious for what lay ahead – the unknown part of it. The 'If I like it, will it mean I'm a lesbian' part of it. And for those of you also thinking this – no, it will not change who you are as a person, or how you think about your sexuality, but it will open you up to the love and purity of yourself. It is so hard to describe and explain but it is not a 'sexual' experience in the way we think of sex; it is just an intense, life changing, personal and transformative experience, which allows the body to open up in ways it has not opened before and to re-align with the pure energy of self.

Kerry is so warm, understanding, supportive and empowering and you feel safe and relaxed from the minute you arrive until the minute you leave. Of which, may I add, you leave feeling totally zen, calm, peaceful and relaxed. The whole experience, and it really is an experience, is heart-felt, purposeful and enjoyable. I don't think future massages will ever compare now as I have experienced the whole body energy shift and a relaxing massage won't be enough for me!

For quite a while now, I have been on an energetic journey but during my session with Kerry, it was the first time I really felt myself as an energetic being rather than a body with energy. I cannot explain how my whole body tingled, pulsed and moved with the energy. I literally felt the energy shift and past traumas release; almost seeing, or sensing, them leave my body. It is really quite an experience. And now, a week after, I feel lighter, more aware and excited for what comes next. Thank you Kerry, for this life-changing experience. Wow, just wow!

Jayne

My life and relationships with my partner and family were in turmoil and I felt overwhelmed, unsupported and just unable to cope. I had my first tantric experience with the beautiful Kerry and, despite being slightly nervous about what to expect, it was quite simply the most moving, nurturing and profound holistic treatment I've ever experienced, and together with some EAM coaching I left her little sanctuary feeling newly enlightened, loved and with a new sense of inner peace.

Annabelle

Kerry is an incredible woman. A few weeks ago I visited her for a tantric experience which was heart opening and mind blowing. I felt so held, supported and accepted by Kerry. On the day, I felt amazing but it's only now that I'm seeing the ripple affect manifesting. I am so much happier with myself and my body. I feel grounded, present, and unshakable every day and this has had a great impact on my relationship and s*x life. Thank you Kerry. Thank you for your wonderful work and being a beautiful person Much love 💕

Leanne

Our first experience of a Tantric Massage as a couple was incredibly powerful!

Having always been quite open to new ideas and learning new techniques within our relationship, we couldn't wait to learn from Kerry

Right from the minute she walked in, we both felt at ease. Having only met Kerry a few times previously, I was quite nervous about how the session would go but that went as soon as she arrived

Her manner, voice and gentle instruction were all calming yet exhilarating. Kerry's knowledge, skills and teaching instruction were very professional yet at the same time, it was like having someone there that we'd known for years and could totally relax with

Kerry made us feel more connected with each other and after 30 years of marriage, I felt such enormous love for my husband. We are now looking forward to practising what Kerry has taught us and experiencing a newfound love, connection and excitement in our relationship.

Couple, Kent

A NOTE FROM AMANDA HEATH - FINE ARTIST, CREATOR OF 'THE GODDESS'

Kerry is someone who is larger than life, and when you meet her, she fills the room with love, joy and possibility. So when she asked me to bring her vision for the cover of the book to life, it was an immediate yes.

I love that from the very beginning, she was clear on exactly the look and feel she wanted and was able to articulate that in detail.

We initially worked through a series of 'drafts', discovering the elements that epitomised the essence of a goddess being awakened. Capturing a resemblance of Kerry and her energy but not an exact likeness as it represents both Kerry's journey and the journey of all the women she reaches through her work.

To have been even a small part of the creation of this book is the greatest blessing, and to have experienced the pure magic of Kerry's energy work myself is something I will never forget.

The painting was created with acrylic, oils and gold leaf and is a symbol of the beauty, possibility, strength and grace that we all hold inside. It suggests that embracing and loving all parts of ourselves, the good, the bad and the ugly, leads to the most phenomenal awakening of the divine feminine.

Meeting and working with Kerry is something I will cherish for ever.

With love and gratitude.

Amanda Heath x

www.ingramcontent.com/pod-product-compliance
Ingram Content Group UK Ltd.
Pitfield, Milton Keynes, MK11 3LW, UK
UKHW021920270726
14059UKWH00006B/154/J